Jonathan Harvey

ARNOLD WHITTALL

Jonathan Harvey

In association with IRCAM

7/461138

faber and faber

First published in 1999
by Faber and Faber Limited
3 Queen Square London WC1N 3AU

Typeset by Faber and Faber Ltd
Printed in England by Clays Ltd, St Ives plc

Music examples reproduced by kind permission of Faber Music Ltd
and Novello & Co Ltd

A CIP record for this book
is available from the British Library

ISBN 0-571-19581-4

10 9 8 7 6 5 4 3 2 1

Contents

Arnold Whittall is well known for his writings on many aspects of nineteenth- and twentieth-century music. Currently Professor Emeritus of Music Theory and Analysis at King's College London, he is a noted broadcaster and reviewer. His recent publications include studies of Berg, Webern, Tippett and Birtwistle.

Preface

I am greatly indebted to Jonathan Harvey for his patience and timely responses to the many queries which I have addressed to him while preparing this handbook. The Interview section has, inevitably, been edited, but every attempt has been made to preserve the spoken quality of the original. To avoid footnotes, certain quotations in the Commentary section are referenced in the text to the (chronological) Bibliography. Other comments by Jonathan Harvey are from notes included with scores or recordings, lectures, or from our interview.

ARNOLD WHITTALL

Interview with Jonathan Harvey

I know that you began to compose at a very early age. Can you say something about your musical background?

It is fitting to start, I think, with my father – not only because he has recently died and I would like to pay tribute to him as the root of everything that has grown in my life, but also because he was in himself a fine composer. For instance, his clarinet quintet was recently played by the Jupiter Ensemble; I have a recording of that performance and I am stunned by the beauty and elegant form of this work, written, I suppose, thirty years ago.

My father was a businessman but an amateur musician. He always regretted that, I think, and would have liked to have been a professional, but the circumstances of his family life would not permit it. He had to support the family firm, a leather-goods factory in Walsall in the industrial Midlands, and he taught himself music; he had piano lessons but virtually nothing in the way of composition lessons. None the less, he would compose in a constant stream throughout most of his life until near the end, and the pieces he wrote were rather short-scale, miniature pieces, often for piano, sometimes for the family or for the circle of musical friends, nearly all amateurs, who would come to visit us for musical evenings. I played the cello, my brother played the violin and had a beautiful voice, and a few friends would come to join us and we would make quartets and piano quintets and trios and so on.

My father wrote in a kind of English mystical pastoral style, incorporating the chromaticism, the subtlety, the darkly shifting elements of continental chromaticism. He loved Skriabin and Fauré, he loved harmonies which were complex and resonant and ways of writing for the piano which would sometimes blur: complex spectral *objets sonores* making for what he would call bell effects. He loved rich and subtle harmony. But he was never given to emotional indulgence. He was a man who hid his emotions, a very private man; and you can hear that in his music, how the subjectivity which seems to peep out behind the landscape is of a reticent sort. It occasionally bursts out, even quite fiercely, but it is somehow subtle and shifting: you can never quite pin it down.

Every evening, when he came home from work, he would play us some of these pieces from around the turn of the century, and he would compose and play some of his own pieces. Sometimes I would follow him, standing by the side of the piano, looking at the music, watching his fingers, even I think from a very early age. And then of course it wasn't long before I had piano lessons, at about the age of six, and started to play myself and with his help to jot a few notes down. Nothing very interesting: but I seemed to have some inclination to do that, which I can't really explain. I think it is this teaching that he gave me, which was entirely unimposing, that I value so much. He never told me what to do in any aspect of life and he never really told me what to do in composing; but he would set an example, just by his spirit, by what I could see he felt, and that would be something I would want to incorporate into myself; genetically no doubt the similarities and the inheritance, the continuity of mind, were there, but I followed his example consciously and he was my favourite composer for many years, my main model.

As a boy you were a chorister at St Michael's College, Tenbury. What was that like?

I went to Tenbury at the age of nine. It was a little choir school founded in the nineteenth century by a professor of music at Oxford University to educate young boys in music and church music, which was then in a state of some decrepitude, not like today. We would sing two services every day, which is more than I think anywhere virtually sings these days, and this wealth of repertoire we encountered was of course extremely educational.

The question remains why it had such a profound effect on me and perhaps not on others; other choristers I know more or less lost interest in music later on. But I think the garden in me that my father had so carefully dug with his presence was receptive to all this music, and things grew; my predilections became quite obsessive and by the time I was eleven I was composing a great deal.

One moment I can remember particularly is turning the corner, coming out of the service to go into the cloisters but still in the church; the organist improvising, playing extremely loudly, full organ, hitting a chord. I used to love his improvisations because I found them more modern – just a hint of chaos – than anything we ever encountered in our singing. And in this particular improvisation – I can't remember the chord any more – there was a moment of great epiphany and I knew that I would always be a composer. And somehow I remembered that for a year, for two years, for ten years, for twenty years, for forty years. It is still clear in my mind.

So I became for some curious reason completely obsessed with composing and I would spend long hours at Tenbury in dingy rooms or sometimes in the magnificent library in the presence of famous manuscripts like Handel's Dublin *Messiah*. I would spend hours and hours sitting at pianos and composing. Some of my music was performed, none of it was much good, but the curious thing, looking back on it, was the state of mind, the absolute joy and delight in shaping sounds which was with me then and of course still is with me. I am not that person now, I have changed completely, I don't recognize any continuity except this same love of living in music – just complete happiness.

At the same time I got to know a lot of music. For instance, I became fanatical about Elgar, and in particular *The Dream of Gerontius*: one of the chaplains gave me a score and I used to go to the piano and play the chromatic 'Dream' motive over and over again. Indeed the whole Prelude was a favourite of mine to play on the piano.

I entered into this strange world of life after death and ghosts and spirits completely. The chapel at St Michael's was often deserted, often dark, when I used to go and practise the organ by myself and I was very aware of strange presences, of ghosts, of all the things that haunt you as a child and you don't understand and you probably dismiss a few years later when reason begins to take its hold upon you. It was a magical world then.

After St Michael's, I went on to Repton and there, having got a musical scholarship, I was of course thrown into the practical business of playing a lot, practising a lot, enjoying my lessons in piano and cello, and the whole process of trying to adapt to a new way of life – very strange. In general I felt very insecure in the first years when I was at the bottom of the pile. Because I happened to like sport, I was not a complete outcast, and that of course brought me together with a lot of other boys and we had a lot of fun in the various games. I didn't feel a kind of freak or misfit with my love of music, which was somewhat unusual, although not unique.

I became less religious than I had been at my choir school, where the rituals had made a deep impression on me. It was a High Anglican atmosphere with plenty of robes and candles, and the celebrations at Christmas and Easter were unforgettably intense. At Repton I abandoned that; I became an atheist, a scientist, a rationalist, a philosopher. Nevertheless, this didn't interfere with the imaginative life of the arts, which remained alive and blazing for me. I was grateful too for the awakenings in Racine, Baudelaire, Mallarmé, Heine, Shakespeare and others in the stimulating literature and language teaching I received there.

After Repton, Cambridge?

I went up to Cambridge in 1957, and went through the usual academic hoops, which I have to say were not terrifically inspiring. The best parts of Cambridge were perhaps the practical parts. There were many good players and again I played a lot of music. I was probably better known as a cellist than a composer and there wasn't all that much time to compose. I got to know a lot of repertoire, chamber music and orchestral music too, and played in the National Youth Orchestra, which was an incredibly uplifting and inspiring experience, up to professional standards of tuning and rhythm and often conducted by excellent people.

What about composition teaching?

I studied composition with Patrick Hadley and that didn't last very long; when I'd been going to his tutorials for about a term and a half, he attacked me for unprepared dissonances and obsessively laid down the law that this was just not a possibility in music. The only thing I could do was to get up and, without a word, rather cross, slam the door and never come back.

But there was light in the compositional teaching in this period for me because I had met Benjamin Britten at Repton and he had been extremely kind to me, had asked to see my compositions, and invited me to Aldeburgh and said very nice encouraging things. I was told that I was a young composer that he was extremely impressed by and this cheered me up a great deal. He found a composition teacher for me. Interestingly enough, it was not a composer but a publisher, a conductor, a Viennese refugee. This was Erwin Stein, who was of course a Schoenberg pupil and a marvellous musician.

I went to see Stein in London every week or every two weeks for about a year and this marvellous, tiny, round man with a very strong, energetic personality put me through the Schoenbergian disciplines of eight-bar structures, sentences and periods, scherzo form, sonata form, just as if I had been starting music at the beginning of my education. He said to me when I arrived, 'Vell, clearly, you are no Mozart.' I think Britten had given him a very rosy picture of me and Stein obviously thought I lacked the traditional disciplines of structure. And he was quite right. I had never seriously thought about eight-bar structures and the inner workings of Beethovenian and Mozartian or indeed Brahmsian phrase structure. So it was very interesting to me to go through all that and Stein allowed me to compose in any style I liked, and I tried all sorts of different harmonic languages, but always with a very clear eight- or other bar structure. If I didn't write in eight-bar structures there had to be a good reason for it. I had to be conscious of going against a natural symmetry.

Unfortunately, in 1958, after this careful disciplined tuition, which had a good effect on tightening my somewhat over-effusive style, Stein died. Britten then thought again and said, 'You perhaps should go to Hans Keller.' He considered a number of English composition teachers but thought none of them acceptable; in fact, he had comically sardonic things to say about most of them in our discussion of this matter. He had of course a very sharp and perceptive tongue.

Be that as it may, he thought Hans Keller would be the best person, continuing this line (which he himself had not been able to follow) of studying with Viennese, Schoenberg-tradition, teachings.

Hans was very different from Erwin Stein. He didn't set me exercises to do each week. He didn't say, 'You must compose every day if you want to be a composer.' He said, 'Bring me your scores as you write them and we will have a talk about them.' And that is exactly what happened. We would meet in a pub (in those days they weren't infested with music); we would drink lavishly – Hans whisky, I usually drank beer, sometimes wine. And during these often hilarious sessions he would psychoanalyse my score, and me too. He would insist that I must compose concretely; there must be no schemes, no automatism, no paper music, no sense really in which the approach was too global. His idea of a strong sense of form was one which was full of violent contrasts, full of the spontaneous, full of the signs of breaking out of form, and somehow form was an unexpected result of almost chaotic intensity. Anathema to him was a unity that was too easily won, which I suppose we would call academic nowadays, a unity too tame and neat.

The crucial experience for him was psychoanalysis and free association: he had been a professional psychoanalyst briefly and had been psychoanalysed. He believed the mind had its own unconscious logic and that this was the essence of art; this was what one had to allow and listen to, and the rational mind should not impose its over-simple dictates on art. Art had to be revelation from this hidden world, otherwise it was banal, and obvious, and we might as well talk words rather than listen to music.

So I always remember this 'lesson', which comes back to me now more and more clearly, though I went away from it for many years. The lesson was: you must think in linear time, not in global time, feeling each moment as the accumulated weight of what has gone before lies upon it. Each moment is composed against the weight of that past, against the patterns that have been established, the energies that you have just heard. It is really an exciting bouncing off what has just occurred. It is not something you can only understand from a global point of view, from above, when it is all finished. You realize, perhaps, there is a certain symmetry, that the blocks match up in some way. No, that is what I *became* interested in, but what he was teaching was the opposite, that at every moment you must feel that tension so that it is absolutely concrete, nothing is abstract. This was the excitement of great music for him, and as it happens you become aware of that perception in the great composers like Haydn and Mozart, whom he admired so much. An enormous inventiveness with a clarity of composition against a background, not in the Schenkerian sense but against a formal implied or stated background of what has been set up already.

After Cambridge you worked on a Ph.D. at Glasgow, and then moved into university teaching. But your own encounters with composer–teachers continued for a while?

In 1966 I encountered Stockhausen at Darmstadt, and in 1969, somewhat incongruously perhaps, I began my book on him at pretty well exactly the same time that I went to Princeton to study with Babbitt. Both Stockhausen and Babbitt were interested in global time: they shared the High Modernist belief that time becomes space, and that one views a musical work, a work of art, as one object, very complex, which should be experienced somehow from above, moving through it but yet conscious of it as a whole, and with no particular sense of line pushing from moment to moment. The logic lies in the enormous planning of the temporal relationships in *Gruppen*, or the serial values in time-points, dynamics, registers and so on in Babbitt's work. These were revolutionary attempts to break down how music was made, how music could be perceived as an almost spiritual dimension, something rising above the material, the stuff of tension, of foreground and background, of composing against, which Hans Keller was propounding. And it is hardly surprising that Hans disapproved both of my Stockhausen book and of my going to study with Babbitt, as indeed did Britten. However, that was the course I pursued and I stayed on it until, I suppose, the late seventies when I began to loosen up, to become less global-time orientated and to listen more to what Hans had taught me before: to go back to his words, having long since ceased to see much of him, yet aware that I had left rather fertile ground.

My reason for going into High Modernism was an urge to find greater structural depth. The early Symphony, *Four Images after Yeats*, *Three Lovescapes*, *Ludus Amoris* and works of that sort were intensely emotional, rather mystical pieces; simply because my aesthetic predilections in the period before I went to study with Babbitt were very strongly influenced by the desire to achieve dark and strong states of intense experience. But I did feel that I needed to reverse the balance and swing the pendulum back a little bit towards classicism, to see if I could find in some of the theories of Stockhausen and Babbitt a way to increase the intricacy of pattern, of perceptible meaning that one draws from the listening experience.

During the 1960s I studied Haydn, Mozart, Beethoven and Schubert particularly in great depth, analysed an enormous number of works, became quite Schenkerian towards the end and began to say, what is the connection between all this and my composing, indeed the composing that I saw all around me in the sixties and seventies? I wanted to find all those levels that I could find in Schenkerian analysis – where are they in contemporary music? If you hear a piece many times, surely you should constantly find new levels which are coherent, all nested one above the other, implicated in the music as it unfolds? I thought that in the serial system I might find this: Babbitt developed it so deeply – there are so many layers – since he himself went through the same process of admiring what Schenker had revealed and realizing one has to make a comparable stab at thinking in similar ways, parallel ways, in our parallel universe of atonal music.

I believe that was mistaken, however, in that it was too intellectual, for me at least. It was not sufficiently audible. It was too dependent on learning. It didn't really take the natural impulses of musical perception, how we connect and what we perceive, sufficiently into account. It involved a forced jump of effort. Sometimes I was able to do that with much preparation, much study of the score, much analysis, with some of Milton's own works, but I could not get as far as I would have liked.

With Stockhausen, of course, it was different and in some ways more complex. He was a composer deep within European tradition, highly emotional, but very scientific, very rational, all at the same time. He could write text pieces, he could write *Gruppen*. And it was this complexity which intrigued me and still does about Stockhausen. Whereas perhaps he was overestimated in those days, now he is very definitely underestimated because the fashion has gone in an opposite direction. But he remains a fascinating model of how to at least make the attempt to bring together the rational, the scientific, the mystical, the intuitive and, let's say, the chaotic. There are many things in Stockhausen which are completely unexplainable except, as he will say, they occurred in one of his dreams. They come from no obvious source.

Of course I responded very much to the spiritual aspects of Stockhausen's work. Global time, somehow living in eternity, I also got from my love of Messiaen at this time. But the aspect of music as space, the aspect of music as physical sound (in the opposite direction), the aspect of music as something you can feel in your fingers when you manipulate sound in an electronic studio, speeding it up, feeling the buttons as they turn, changing the sound, getting inside sound, getting to understand and love the graininess, the smoothness, the richness, the roughness, the thinness of the ontology of musical sound – Stockhausen showed me all these things very intensely and has remained a mysterious guide in my work.

*Before we pursue compositional matters, could you say a bit
more about your experience as a teacher?*

My first post at university level was at Southampton University
and this stretched from 1964 to 1977. I was allotted the First and
Second Viennese schools and in between Wagner, Bruckner and
Mahler. I would not have chosen the First Viennese school because
I had viewed myself as more naturally attuned to later styles, but
there was a gap in the teaching so I took it on and in the event it
turned out of course to be a continuation of what Erwin Stein and
Hans Keller had been talking about. I also introduced a class on
Schenker, which was quite early to do so in Britain, though in the
United States this type of study had been going for some years.

I also introduced courses where modernist composers like Boulez
and Ligeti were made familiar to the students, although inevitably
when history is taught chronologically there is only a tiny little time
at the end of the year left by the time you have got through all you
are keen to get through in the previous generations.

Also at Southampton I taught composition, and I particularly
liked the undergraduate classes where I would take fifteen or twenty
people in workshops, and I would teach them individually too. But
in the group sessions, the studies and exercises we worked out we
would perform ourselves: there was a tremendous sense of immediate feedback for the students, and for me too. Sometimes I would
pick up ideas, a little sound pattern or shape would occur which
would actually in some form or other find its way into my thinking.

There were some of us who were very keen on improvisation
and even in those days in the sixties we were using electronics – in
the late sixties anyway and early seventies – and I remember we
would improvise for two whole days; except for the break for a
night's sleep. Such changing of consciousness was very powerful.
You come out of the end of two days of improvisation and all the
sounds that you hear in the world have a totally different meaning
for you. I suppose this is what Cage's ideal would have been when
he wanted us to forget music and to hear sound. Or perhaps it is
the opposite of what Cage meant. I don't know. He said that the

only people who couldn't listen to his music properly were musicians. But be that as it may, everything, all street sounds, had been converted into our music. That is certainly the way it appeared to us for the weeks following such improvisations.

In 1977 you moved from Southampton to Sussex.

Sussex University was – is – an inter-disciplinary university and the music students for half their time study an 'umbrella' of other subjects – perhaps a geographical area, like English and American, or European, or a thematic grouping as in Cultural and Community Studies, where I operated. I would teach courses to do with art and the spiritual, with Marxism taken on board. We would try to reinstate the transcendental – or at least *I* would – which was somewhat excluded by Marxist sociological thought, and try to find the mysterious dimension of release from one's historically determined position: how it is possible to conceive of such a notion, and the autonomy of art, and so on. I would teach another course on twentieth-century opera from similar perspectives.

What about composition teaching at Sussex?

I was fortunate to have some marvellously interesting composition students and I learned a lot from them. Exchanges of ideas, imaginative sessions. Of course, many teachers say you can't teach composition and yet very often they are the ones that spend the longest hours with their composition students. So I don't know what they do, if not teaching. It is an exchange. It is a kind of thing which can't be quantified. Perhaps that is why people say it can't be taught at all, which is nonsense. It can't be measurably taught but it can be qualitatively taught. There is a certain quality of relationship, a kind of intuitive osmosis going on in a good composition session, I believe. Of course a teacher can make suggestions, technical ones are perfectly teachable, as everybody knows, but, more deeply: suggestions about the aesthetics, the spirituality of the work, and the student will react to that, possibly in the opposite direction – who cares? Perhaps a strength will build up against this sounding board which is the composition teacher.

Quite recently you've moved from Sussex to Stanford, California.

Well, Sussex – like so many British universities – became overrun with managerial and administrative forces, and so I felt very uncomfortable. The improvisatory quality of teaching had vanished and things were much more laid down on pieces of paper and syllabuses and assessments, just like a business really, and I decided to leave. After I had got myself into a frame of mind where I would begin to enjoy an early retirement in a somewhat impoverished state, I had a phone call from John Chowning at Stanford asking whether I would be interested in a composition post there. My function was obviously to be a member of the Music Department, a composition professor, and yet have one foot in the Centre for Computer Research into Music and Acoustics – CCRMA, or Karma, as it is always called. The Centre is up on the hill a couple of hundred yards away from the Music Department in a most beautiful flower-surrounded building with the danger that it could be a little bit separate from the Music Department. And I accepted the job; I was very pleased to forge close links again between 'traditional' musicians and the engineers, the programmers, the computer composers, the composers who use computers (who are slightly different). It's a paradise of a place and the atmosphere is conducive to hard work and interchange of ideas. I found it very fertile from the point of view of students helping me and teaching me in new computer developments, and me helping them with their compositions and trying to get over the snare of being trapped by technology, which happens to some people: they become too engrossed in the processes themselves to remember what it is really like to be driven by purely aesthetic musical impulses.

I teach mostly composition there. I learn a lot from projects which we do in the seminar – it is an international gathering of composers, small but distinguished; for instance one project was each week to bring rhythms which we would tap on the table in the middle of the seminar room, and no matter how complex (and many of the composers tended to be rather mathematical and rather systematic in approach) I insisted they had to be able to perform their own rhythms, which was very revealing. And I think they learned a lot. Of course they would write duets, trios, quartets and so on and so we would all be involved in trying to master complex rhythmic notation; and trying to simplify that notation without simplifying the musical thought was one of the tasks of the project.

At Stanford I have learned a lot from the oriental perspectives of many of the students, from Korea or Japan or Taiwan or China. They have rather different views about time and about drama. Music is often rather pictorial and often very static and ritualistic. I suppose one might expect this but to get inside their minds is a fascinating challenge for me, though in general my policy is to get them to bounce their ideas off me and I will say, 'I would do it like this,' and see in what way they object. By this dialectical process we gradually find out what they really want.

I'd now like to look a little more closely at the ideas and beliefs that have informed your creative work. What particular spiritual and religious qualities concern you?

As someone with Buddhist tendencies, particularly at this stage of my life, I enjoy looking back on my life with the kind of rather objective question: why does one person have predilections this way and another that way? What is the nature of Karma? What is the mental continuum that continues through the process of reincarnation? Is there such a thing as reincarnation? These are questions which fascinate me and I can see, looking back, that I did have certain predilections. Where they came from is what fascinates me. These predilections were towards mysticism and transcendental experience. When I was young, I had a propensity for solitude – I suppose many adolescents do, but I used to spend many long hours in the countryside wandering alone, which actually I don't remember any of my friends doing, and I would of course be buried in music, I would usually be singing to myself; and when I wasn't walking alone in the countryside I would be playing from my father's huge record collection.

At Cambridge I became very absorbed, quite suddenly, in mystical writing, like that of St John of the Cross. Christian mysticism seemed to lead out of a framework that I knew and understood fairly well into a more general, more heterodox consciousness, which of course had many resonances in oriental religion. Someone said, 'You only have to squeeze St John of the Cross like a sponge and you are left with pure Buddhism.' The experiences were enhanced by visits to monasteries, where I would stay a few days; usually lonely, quiet, peaceful places. And I would sense, particularly in the faces of those who lived there, something special. It is curious that it was in the faces – also in the rituals but particularly in the faces – that I felt one of the deepest messages I had yet received was to be descried. In many ways faces teach us more than books, art or anything else.

When did you first encounter Rudolf Steiner's writings?

In about 1972. A friend told me about him and I read I think forty books there and then over about a year and a half. And it was a complex impression; it is hard to say exactly in a few words what Steiner gave, but it was the spiritual nature of everything I saw around me which he somehow drew out. Being a Goethe scholar, he believed one should start with the generality and finish with the detail, whereas modern scientific method is exactly the opposite: you look at details and you try to end up with an abstract general principle, which in a way reduces the vividness of the immediate detailed entity. With Steiner and Goethe, the other world view was important, ending up with a special view of the ordinary things of life, of people, of objects, of nature, minerals, animals, vegetable nature – everything one saw around one had its spiritual nature, its own place in this clairvoyantly perceived universe of light and colour and vibration. Steiner could see all this and – one had to take this on trust – he was a clairvoyant who saw light, who saw the classic mystical vision of the great masters recorded throughout the centuries from all time, of the universe's light. Every object can be dissolved into a kind of other nature, showing its impermanence, its total emptiness, as Buddhists would say.

Steiner talked about wonderful worlds which were poetically very resonant for me, worlds of light and colour and sound, which he said 'we visit in our dream state and which we also pass through between two incarnations'. It is a life between two spells on this Earth or wherever else we incarnate. I picked up on quite a lot of this in my opera, *Inquest of Love*, of which the basic theme is what happens after death, or what can happen, or what did happen to a particular triangle of human beings, and how the conflicts of their lives were to some extent resolved in a different dimension. But that's another story.

Steiner had an impact on my music, by dissolving some of the clear classical formalities into more impressionistic textures, perhaps closer to French music, to Debussy – what Boulez (approvingly) and Adorno (somewhat disapprovingly) called 'phantasmagoria'. This is the kind of sound world which moves away from the neatness of discourse, of statement, of argument and instates another kind of music-world which is that of living in sound, not particularly defined by argument and logic but just as a particularly intense state of being.

I found this all very exciting but later on another important defining moment was my encounter with a very special way of achieving some of those states. Of course I don't claim to have reached anything like the clairvoyance and vision of someone like Steiner, who was unusually gifted, but with an ancient Vedic technique of meditation which I learned through transcendental meditation, I was able to install in my daily routine a discipline, a practice, which would at least put me on the path. I felt I could make progress; it was not too demanding and I could stick to it, and from time to time it led me to have experiences of transcendence which were very formative in my musical writing. In particular, silence began to become more prominent in my music, and near-silence, and also long sounds which were static and rather empty – the concept of emptiness again.

'Transcendence' is a word you use a lot. How would you define it?

One can't describe what pure transcendence is; it is beyond knowledge; it is a zero; but the borderlands of transcendence are exactly what art is about and it is quite clear what these borderlands are. Sometimes you are just on the edge of transcendence, other times you are somewhere within the region and that is quite easy to describe because it has a lot of connections with the normal states of consciousness we move in day by day, so it can be mediated in those terms. Once one has a clear idea of what is at the basis of art, although art can never actually say it, I think it can induce such experiences in people by suggestion and encouragement: one can then see more clearly the aim of art and where to go, and life becomes very exciting at that point.

Winchester Cathedral was clearly an important place for you
in this connection.

After my son Dominic went to be a chorister at Winchester, my wife Rosa and I used to go there very regularly and immerse ourselves in that wonderful building, often in the darkness of a winter's evening, and hear one of the great choirs (a boys' choir with lay clerks) of England, conducted by Martin Neary, who is a fantastic musician. And also Martin would encourage me to write for the choir and I think I have over the years amassed some twelve or fifteen works for that type of choir. I enjoyed being part of a communal expression. These works would be performed; I would not have to take a bow; they would be part of an act of communal worship. My success or failure would be assessed solely in terms of how much I had contributed to the worship, how much I had moved people, how much the music had transcended me and become one with the contemplation of the texts of the moment. This was liberating. It helped me to forget all personal ambition (or at least move in that direction) and I enjoyed writing for that mysterious acoustic where everything is blended over about two or three seconds, so any changes of chord run into each other; and it was fascinating to explore the extraordinary Romanesque and Gothic spaces with these sounds and hear them hit the surfaces and bounce back as if the whole place is coming alive. When one was listening to simple chanting of prayers, perhaps on one or two notes, one would hear very strongly a halo of harmonics ringing out. Some harmonics were particularly resonant in the higher region and this seemed to give something beyond the merely individual voice, as if the building itself were singing, or contributing. It was a reaching out beyond the individual into this communal expression, which was an important aesthetic and spiritual lesson for me.

In 1981 they performed the church opera *Passion and Resurrection*, a kind of culmination of our collaboration, together with the collaboration of the Dean, who was extremely sympathetic and visionary about the place of music, also of poetry and dance, in the cathedral, a quite extraordinary man, very austere but very spiritual. Also there was Bishop Taylor, who has become a very close friend, who is quite simply one of the most remarkable men I have ever known. He produced the opera and for a prominent bishop engaged in politics and running the diocese this was a very brave and typically individualistic thing for John Taylor to do. He believed the Church should tell the ancient stories in new ways and make them immediate and alive. And so we worked together on the story of the Passion and Resurrection, taking texts from Benedictine Latin liturgical dramas, and the whole process of getting it up was again a community one, for the community of Winchester; many hundreds of people were involved in one way or another and the whole rehearsal period was prefaced by the ritual of Eucharist taken together.

That was the spirit in which it progressed. Constantly searching for meaning, questioning what all the extraordinary events of this story meant. It was a wonderfully high time. I found music for the first part, 'Passion', that was rather austere and quite cruel and brutal, while for 'Resurrection' I based the music, for the first time, on symmetrical inversion. The harmony seemed to leave its bass structures and radiate out from a central point, an axis in the middle which remained constant, giving a kind of floating effect which I think suited the liberation from history, the liberation from the past, the making of a new era which the Resurrection portends for Christians.

That was a wonderful period and the mystical Christ remains with me very much to this day. But I have gradually become more Buddhist and that again is a defining moment for me. More and more in recent works I take the ideas of Buddhism, of sutra and tantra, and put them into my music. *Forms of Emptiness* for choir, for instance, takes a setting of the Heart Sutra – not a setting, but just a chant, because I would not presume really to set music to this ancient austere text, which is about the emptiness of form. And against it I put some e.e. cummings poems, which are like flashes of impermanence, colour and passing vision thrown up against the austere meditation on the emptiness, the lack of existence of anything in its own right.

There's an obvious question at this point. How is it possible
to link these very profound and longstanding spiritual concerns
with the concrete specifics of modern compositional techniques
– serialism, spectralism, and so on?

For me, there is a certainly a direct connection, and technique is simply a tool, a means for the expression of the other. For example, serialism became really more of a harmonic thing for me, rather than a method of spinning out lines of notes or polyphonies. By harmonic, I mean more the kind of thing that can occasionally be found in Schoenberg and Webern, and also Boulez. They will set up what are often twelve-note harmonic fields, then explore the symmetrical recurrence of harmonic types. Series are moved through in combinatorial conjunctions, taking the harmonic axial symmetry which results from the combination of prime and inversion, or the combination of several primes and inversions, and the composer examines how the symmetrical parade of intervals systematically created from this can reflect a certain axial symmetry and release from bass functions.

Bass functions in my mind came to be associated with the nineteenth century, also the seventeenth and eighteenth centuries, of course, but essentially the world of emotional individualistic expression, whereas this more objective music was a little more cosmic. Again, I thought of oriental parallels, of symmetrical modes, and of Renaissance and medieval music which is less centred and emotionally dependent on some tonic. The sense of community in those cultures, whether in fact true or not, seemed to me to be a parallel to the act of leaving that obsession with individual identity put forward by nineteenth-century music.

All that still interested me very much instinctively and intuitively but I wanted to solve a problem. To put it very simply, it was the problem of suffering, and it still is. This seems to me the most important problem, in fact the only problem which one should be engaged with: in art as in life, what is suffering and what is the key to alleviating it or even eliminating it? It leads back to Buddhism. Buddha is of course famous for proposing just such a solution and it seems his whole life was engaged in the Bodhisattva mission of alleviating suffering, bringing enlightenment and releasing all beings, all living beings from samsara, the world of suffering. Be that as it may, I certainly felt that this more objective music was in the direction of moving away from this fascinating world of samsara, of suffering, in which we are interminably caught and upon which art endlessly meditates. Great art is cathartic and to some extent does alleviate suffering by confronting suffering in the most tragic works. Nevertheless I think we would not feel it is great art unless there is something revealed beyond and above that suffering, some other dimension to it than just itself.

It's clear that the representation of symmetry as stable and in this sense dissolving the tensions of suffering is fundamental to your thinking. Can you say a little more about the musical consequences of this?

Symmetrical fields would be radiating out in intervals that mirrored each other from a central axis and often there would be other axes set up at symmetrical points in the ascent or the descent from that central axis. So you can take the high music and it would have its own central axis, and the low music would also have its own central axis, and the high music could mirror the low music exactly. Or the two halves of the low music could mirror each other, or the two halves of the high music could mirror each other. And sometimes there were many more than just the three points of axis I have suggested there. So these symmetries created symmetrical worlds which were repertoires through which I could, as it were, pour my melodic and harmonic thinking. They were sieves through which the music was pressed. They enabled me to write rather easily and rather fast and they ensured coherence. I would set up a few fields for each piece – maybe eight, five, ten, something like that – each one with its own feeling, with its own nature, its own spirit, its own grain, its own dissonance, its density or its thinness.

For instance, in the work I have just at the moment of speaking finished, these fields suggest all sorts of formal possibilities. I have become very interested in canon and the work I have just finished is entirely canonic. The work is called *Calling Across Time* and I wrote it for the opening of the new British Library. I thought of course of books, in part, calling to us across time and across the continents. And a music is played in one part of the orchestra which is repeated in canon at a certain interval which guarantees that the entire music will be part of the same harmonic field; in other words, the harmonic field reduplicates itself every so often. Taking a chunk of this harmonic field and putting it down a fourth reduplicates all the same intervals, for instance, or down a seventh or a minor ninth, or whatever.

And also there is a certain atonality. Enough notes are included within a reasonable span of register to avoid it sounding like C major or some tonality; there is an appealing atonality which is not particularly dissonant but yet which is its own world, if not a tonal one. So using these kinds of fields I am able to throw elaborate canons into motion in mensurated form; they copy each other at different speeds, the second voice playing at a faster speed than the first, so it eventually overtakes it and takes the lead. This kind of thing I like very much, the moment of overtaking and all that that implies in terms of musical structure. So these fields can be

used either rather freely or exactly to engender precise forms born from their nature.

I think the symmetrical fields and harmonies are able to capture states of consciousness which are achieved in meditation or in samadhi or, as I say, to encourage them in people because of their self-contained floating nature. I felt there was a relationship between the imagination and the technique here. It is not, I hope, an indulgent, New Age at its worst, sort of escapist music that I have sought, one which just floats in some soothing hot bath of happiness, but something rather more intense. The word 'bliss' crops up in most of the mystical writers, people who have achieved something in meditation and in samadhi. Bliss is an ultimate – in fact the most wonderful thing that human beings can possibly know. But it is not, I think, the purpose of art generally to bathe in this, in unalloyed form – it is perhaps not possible anyway. It has to be mediated with the imperfect instruments and possibilities of human resources. In any case my aesthetic is more that of including the whole personality, that if a state of consciousness is present in the music it must be related to the struggle to achieve that state of consciousness. Not just that mind but the mind of reason, the mind of form, the mind of conflict, the mind of dialectic, the mind of suffering – all these are thrown into perspective on the screen of bliss. They are projected there but ultimately we see the whiteness of the screen itself as well, I hope. All these are melted into light. The unity of vision which springs from the realization that nothing has its own existence, that everything is changing, that the tangle of cause and effect is absolutely interminable and incomprehensible, and what we take as the ego, the hard and strong entity, is in fact illusory. Once these things are a little bit clearer and related to the state of meditation consciousness, then it is possible for art, I think, to reflect the toing and froing, the dialectic between such form and such emptiness. It is the unity and not cheap unity, not academic unity, but unity of profound experience which is in my view at the base of everything that I would find great. I realize this if I ask myself the question what art appears to me as great and analyse my reasons and I come up with that conclusion.

*So far you've talked primarily about harmony, but structuring
in terms of melody is also a crucial factor in your work.*

With an electronic work, *Ritual Melodies*, which I started in 1985,
I combined sixteen melodies into a chain. I did this because up to
that point I had been working largely with quasi-serial cells,
germs, small structures which would form different melodic and
linear continuities and never particularly congeal into a well-made
melody, so to speak. I began to see that it was difficult to perceive
the identity of such material and it was not strong enough to build
form very clearly. I wanted something more memorable so that
when it recurred after a long absence – after so many minutes – it
would still be recognizable, therefore form is present. If you don't
recognize it, there is no form. If it is played simultaneously with
several different melodies, different musical activities, it is still recognizable, it is a strong enough shape and personality. Therefore
melodies are necessary for polyphony and form to be really exciting, to have more meaning, to have depth of meaning and richness
of structure. A lot of complex music nowadays is of course quite
simple because there is a lot going on but none of it is memorable
enough to make the complexity have many different, quantifiable
items within it. It becomes one complex item.

So these sorts of reasons led me to build systematic melody
chains. I would take a melody and construct against it a second
melody which would, as it were, fill in the gaps, or the long notes,
with its characteristic gestures, trills, movements, ornaments,
whatever made it distinctive. And so there we would have what I
would call Melody A and Melody B and, in the middle, AB, which
would be a new melody, a composite one, composed of the two
old ones. It was a more busy melody, of course; it combined the activities of the first and instead of having gaps or long notes it
would go into the activities of the second. In this way large webs
of polyphony could be built up of precisely congruent melodies
slotting into each other, not just A with B, but A with B with C
with D, and so on. And the timing could be measured precisely by
the computer, perhaps to a greater degree than with the instru-

mental works in which I tried the same technique. But the timing was very precise so even the quickest notes could borrow from each other's melodies and intersperse one note from one melody and another note from another melody. And the whole thing in *Ritual Melodies* was unified by belonging to one harmonic series. The partials used were six to forty, and those thirty-five partials were the sole content of the melodies. Sometimes they would be transposed up a few harmonics but they would always use the same rungs of the ladder, so to speak, to move around on. That meant that each interval was different, no two intervals are the same in the harmonic series, and it was unified in the way that I have been talking about; although the melodies were full of rhythms and trills and dotted rhythms and glissandi and so on, they nevertheless belonged to a larger whole of which they were fairly obviously just a part. And this whole stayed put pretty well for the entire thirteen and a half minutes of the piece; there was no change from this one harmonic series which gave the repertoire of pitches – so it was like a great arpeggiation.

I used that technique in a number of works and still resort to it from time to time, trying to achieve a polyphony and a relationship between melodies of closeness or distance which I think of as a kind of kinship chart (some melodies are brothers, others are distant cousins) and you can modulate using these intervals of kinship through the melodies, one by one, through the close family relationships, or of course you can jump right out and see a distant member of the family, which can be a bit of a shock, a striking contrast, in other words.

All the usual intervals of composition are present in this systematic way of thinking of melodies. The art was to make melodies so that they were well formed both as simple melodies and as composite melodies. When you add two melodies together, you don't necessarily get a good form in itself. The two separate melodies must be so composed that when added together they achieve each other, the shapes and impulses within the movement of the line up and down and the rhythmic energies are meaningful as one Gestalt, as one composite melody.

So once that is all worked out (and it is a kind of pre-compositional thing, although there is a lot of emotional subjectivity involved in such invention as well), then the piece can be made with that material. In the case of *Ritual Melodies*, the melodies were all set in the form of numbers in the computer and it was largely a matter of just placing them by pressing the right buttons for the right figures and putting them in time, the right durations, the right juxtapositions.

By the time you were working on Ritual Melodies *at IRCAM you'd already had considerable experience of working in studios. Can you fill in this background a little?*

Perhaps my first introduction to electronic music was at Princeton, working at computer music in the course that was offered when I was there in 1969–70. I developed a love for the sounds through the works of Stockhausen – *Gesang der Jünglinge, Kontakte, Telemusik* – and these were the subject of my thoughts as I went to Princeton, writing a book on Stockhausen and also working with Babbitt. But I was unable to continue computer music studies in England. The facilities were few and difficult to manage, but I worked in several electronic studios, notably that at Cardiff University, which was well developed with analogue synthesizers, and I created the *Inner Light* series. But it was not really until 1980, when I was invited to work at IRCAM, that my thinking was able to develop in a more coherent way.

The pleasure of at last finding the means to realize one's ideas was intense: IRCAM was a gift from God (in the form of Pierre Boulez!). I worked there with the encouragement of Boulez, Nicholas Snowman and Tod Machover and, as is the marvellous way at IRCAM, one is given the help of tutors, people who live there, know the system from day-to-day contact, and can help someone coming in from the outside quickly to engage with what interests them. Stanley Haynes, who had been a student of mine in England, was there and he was one of the first to help me. Denis Lorrain, Jean-Baptiste Barrière, who is still there and is a very eminent, stimulating, revolutionary thinker, are marvellous people to discuss one's ideas with. One goes to IRCAM, one has long discussions with people like Barrière, and this helps to refine the ideas, hearing about what other people have done, seeing how ideas might be possible – not only that, but how they might be extended and developed beyond what one had thought of. This is why IRCAM is so valuable. I worked with Xavier Rodet, Jan Vandenheede and Cort Lippe on my later pieces, and they all fulfilled extremely valuable functions, not just technically helping me to realize what I had in my mind, but as composers themselves, people to discuss with and bounce ideas off and to receive their ideas. Very important.

At first IRCAM was a curious place. It was intensely exciting, but quite dark in some ways, full of conflicts and tensions. Boulez was up against tremendous opposition. He had made this grand gesture of heroic defiance, I think, in getting Pompidou to pour all this money into a project whose validity many French people doubted; in fact many people internationally doubted, and I think the burden of proof was heavy on his shoulders. Standards had to be intense; there was a kind of enclosed idealism, a kind of, as I say, defiance about the place then. It was not so open and smiling to the public; it was out to develop something which Boulez suspected – well, *knew*, because he is a genius at seeing distant targets – was of immense importance for the future of music, but at that time it was by no means obvious. So there was a kind of darkness in IRCAM and I felt a little afraid going there, but I was comforted by the familiarity of the sounds I took with me, of my son and the Winchester bell, with which to work in this atmosphere. And there were many wonderful, nice people there, some of whom I've mentioned already. But one had to work very hard (of course that was no problem) in underground studios and live an intense round-the-clock creative life, which was pretty exhausting.

As the years went on and I went back, somehow the tensions became less necessary; the place justified itself. People seemed more relaxed. The concert life became quite celebrated, as the Ensemble InterContemporain grew more and more into the present reputation it enjoys. Boulez and others gave wonderful concerts, every week; Boulez and Messiaen would give seminars and lectures; many other people gave lectures; composers would float in to see what was going on or spend a few days trying something out; and one met extraordinary people all the time. It was a real centre, one had a sense that music was centring in on this place on the earth, and going back again to take some of the inspiration to Japan, China, Korea, America, Europe, the Middle East – wherever.

Nowadays it is very open to the public; masses of people know about it; it has a smiling exterior; the public is no problem. I think the only problem probably is with some politicians and with the flow of money. This is perhaps to be expected; there are many conflicts and social issues which arise in French economics and politics, and these are the only tensions nowadays. It seems to be a much more open place; everything is involved in 'pedagogy', both at a very high advanced level, where a few select people are chosen each year to study intensively, and at an intermediate level, where there are week-long courses and short courses or weekends, and at a mass level, where the public, curious as ever in French culture, comes to see what these programs can do and buys them for their own domestic computer use and learns and enjoys.

Your first three works at IRCAM were Mortuos plango, Bhakti *and* Ritual Melodies. *You've already talked about the third from the point of view of its melodic structures. Can you now say something a little more generally about all three pieces, and about 'spectralism'; something we hear a good deal about today.*

There's a kind of spectralism in *Ritual Melodies*, the whole work based on one spectrum. This was also present in *Mortuos plango*, my first work for IRCAM in 1980, one of the early works for that institution.

Mortuos plango was based on the spectrum of a Winchester Cathedral bell, and the voice of my son Dominic, then a Winchester chorister, is the other component of the dialectic of the piece. It's a meditation on bell and boy and 'morphing' (as the current term is, though it didn't exist in those days) between the two spectra, between the two types of sound. It's an unfolding of this bell spectrum (which is an inharmonic structure, not a harmonic series): throughout the eight sections of the piece a different part of the structure is explored, a different prominent partial is taken as central partial, and new spectra (which are simply transpositions of the original bell spectrum) are built up and modulated between by glissandi on the partials. So I would modulate from one bell to another, from a bigger bell to a smaller bell, by a process of sliding sine tones in the computer. This was modulatory spectralism, and spectralism has grown in importance in my thinking immensely since those days. It was of course a gesture towards integration and spectralism remains, perhaps, the most important grammar at the end of musical evolution in this century.

There are similar features in my second IRCAM work, *Bhakti*, particularly in the ninth movement. The pitch structure of *Bhakti* is rigorously combinatorial, intensively serial, using techniques derived from Milton Babbitt and his teaching, which I had encountered, of course, in 1969–70 in Princeton, but have used in symmetrical harmonic fields. So this manipulation of combinatorial series was always subject to the feel of the harmonic series, to the coloration, as it were, which is, I think, rather different from how Milton approaches it. However, one of the processes of this serialism was the assembly and disassembly of the twelve pitch classes, and *Bhakti* starts from one – which is actually G, rises to twelve, and comes back to one. And when it comes back to one, I have an extended meditation on one note: I developed with the help of the IRCAM tutors an elaborate three-minute movement of spectral exploration of this harmonic series on G. It was a very low G, the one which lies below the bottom of the piano, and the thousands of partials which are clearly audible above that were filtered in a way not unlike the way we filter partials when we make vowel forms in speech: each vowel is, of course, a different formation of loudnesses, of amplitudes, and when we make a diphthong we make a shift of the filter in our mouths, in our nasal and vocal cavities. It is exactly the same in this movement of *Bhakti* but all done synthetically by synthetic sine tones.

When you are dealing with spectral matters you become very aware, in the studio and elsewhere, of the dialectic between fusion and fission – that sounds can be part of a whole. And they are so much a part of that whole that you can't distinguish them any more as parts; they somehow blend like a chameleon into the whole; they lose their individuality. But the fascination is in the hide-and-seek process where sounds which you took to be individual, highly characterized sounds, identities, instruments, whatever, can hide themselves and blend so perfectly you can't see them any more. They come in and out of identity. They are highly individual beings and yet they are also empty, lacking inherent existence, just part of some whole. And when this process occurs often enough, in and out, hidden and revealed, we have a kind of mystical essence of music which I think is very important; I would not dismiss it as illusion in the way Adorno does, as some kind of lesser phantasmagoric reality. For me, it is the very nature of reality itself – that behind individuality one discerns a unity. And that is heard all the time in spectral music and that's the fascination of it.

That is so even in a work like *Tombeau de Messiaen* for such hard-nosed individuals as concert piano, and tape, where on the tape are just piano sounds, almost completely. There are some gong sounds but mostly it is composed of recorded piano sounds. But they are recorded in a spectral formation. Instead of the pianos on the tape playing the normal tempered tuning, they play only in natural harmonic series. And these micro-intervallic harmonic series are played at the same volume as the normally tuned live piano, so the live piano seems to belong to the harmonic series and it becomes part of a unified structure. But then it also has notes every now and again which are out of tune, or more often than that, and it completely leaves the membership of the harmonic series, so it becomes something in dialectic, in argument with the fused nature of the harmonic series. Thus such a way of thinking in and out of fusion has determined the structure of a piece like that.

But there are more obvious examples. The use of electronics with instruments – say, in ensemble works or orchestral works like

Madonna of Winter and Spring – that usage is often in the same direction: the electronics are not used very much to define sharp individual gestures and moments, as in some composers' work; they are more used to provide the backwash, the texture, the harmonic fields, the fused object into which the defined instruments of the orchestra blend. A typical process would be for the orchestra to dissolve into a static sound and lose its identity. For instance, in *Madonna of Winter and Spring* there is a considerable use of live reverberation, so the orchestra plays a few seconds of music in a certain harmonic field, the reverberator picks that up through a microphone and then shuts off the input and continues to put out that reverberated second or two of music as a constant static sound. So it is, as it were, the static underlying ground of the orchestra which continues. The orchestra might go on to other things or it might linger a while in this static continuum, this state of unity. And then it may break out of it. Eventually in that piece the whole work comes to a timeless halt and just the sounds that are reverberated from earlier music are heard in a kind of unchanging continuum, with small differentiated features cycling round within it.

Electronics, then, has a very important role, not only in the growth of spectralism, which is so revolutionary and so crucial in the development of music today, but also in its own right as an extension of timbre, and also of speed, making it possible for music to be faster or slower than ever before. These things – and also the sheer joy of playing with identity, how a clarinet can turn into something else, maybe into a trombone or maybe something completely ridiculous, but also the transformation, the blurring of the edges that had been established in previous music: these are among the great explorations of our time.

Could you say something about your experiences in studios other than IRCAM?

One was at the Massachusetts Institute of Technology, where I produced *From Silence*. Again this was a very highly advanced institute of computer music. Tod Machover and Barry Vercoe were there.

And, again perhaps, I had the same impulse to bring into a highly computerized and technological world at MIT material of some incongruity. I went with some texts which were written by the abbess of an abbey in Kent near where I live, which I visited, and they are rather beautiful short mystical meditations; and then I composed some texts myself in conjunction with composing the music, and these are perhaps more Buddhist-orientated. The critic of the *Boston Globe*, Richard Dyer, referred to me, in his review of my piece, as a 'curiously medieval figure', which pleased me very much.

At any rate, I enjoyed working at MIT and we integrated soprano, acoustic instruments and electronic instruments together in one spiritual world. I wanted to make a piece in this case which used a lot of fairly simple techniques and put them together, actually making quite a complex set-up, and treatments – live treatments, short recorded sounds, longer recorded sounds, played back either by sampler or tape, depending on the length of the sounds, soprano and violin treated live.

Another studio I enjoyed working in was the Westdeutscher Rundfunk (WDR) in Cologne. This was the studio that Stockhausen had been Director of and the ghost of Stockhausen still hovered over it. In fact he still works there. But it was the scene of the famous *Gesang der Jünglinge*, *Kontakte*, and so on; all the classic Stockhausen masterpieces came from this studio.

Whether it was for that reason or not, I wanted to research the acceleration of rhythm, which was a famous preoccupation of Stockhausen. Using the Fairlight they had, I could accelerate the speed of certain rhythmic cells until they became pitches, the rhythms became notes. According to the nature of the rhythmic accentuation-structure they would have different timbres, different colours, and different partials would be predominant according to the frequencies thrown up by accelerating rhythm. In metaphysical terms this meant that the rhythms of the physical world, of the body, of the dance, of gesture, became speeded up until they became steady stasis; dance became stasis when it became so fast and beyond that it shot off into the stratosphere and became a kind of colour or texture, something not quite the same as pitch. And that

I regard as a kind of transcendence, going into a high static empty sound, quite close to silence.

So the dialectic here was between body rhythm and transcendence and with all the stages in between. The piece – *One Evening* – is quite Buddhist in that it uses two singers, a soprano and a mezzo-soprano, and they sing texts related to emptiness. The first one is a Chinese Buddhist's text about an experience of emptiness he had 'like moonlight on snow', as he described it, and it is a very white sort of movement, with reverberant struck sounds both on the purely electronic side and from the treated percussion and harp.

The second movement is a vision of unity from Rabindranath Tagore, whose poems I had also used in *Song Offerings*. I use a text from a letter in which he describes an experience of rhythmic light, the same theme that I have talked about before, to do with the unity of people and objects, the scene he saw from the balcony of his house in a town, when the scene dissolved and became rhythmic light. Everything became united in one dance.

The third movement was from an American writer who didn't want to be named: an experience of horrific fear from lack of self. It is the twentieth-century version of emptiness which you get in Samuel Beckett and many other twentieth century masters; the *horror vacui*, the sense that we are nothing, that we have been completely deconstructed, we only consist of our history and our context and there is no self – which is, of course, a Buddhist truth, but there is a horrific fearful side to this which has been predominant in our century, and here it was experienced by this lady as a very real terror.

The fourth movement is the classic Buddhist marriage of bliss and emptiness. It just takes a little bit of Sanskrit text in praise of the all-compassionate emptiness and sings endlessly the same kind of rhythms, dancing with tabla accompaniment basically; repeating over and over again in a kind of trancelike state the bliss of emptiness. So that was, I felt, a not inappropriate theme for the Stockhausen studio, and indeed Stockhausen came to the performance and said many wonderful things to me afterwards. I was very happy about that.

Over the years you've worked with many kinds of performer.

This is one of life's great pleasures – to leave one's lonely study and bring the fruits of one's labour to sympathetic people who are eager to make them live. The human experiences are so rich – the joint exploration of wonder and magical happenings, the exhilaration, the laughter, the jokes: often without it ever being mentioned, one 'lives in' the work unconsciously as a community.

Musicians like Martin Neary with his choirs, Frances-Marie Uitti with her cello, and the Arditti Quartet have all inspired me with their dedicated love of beauty and wonderment: I have written much for all of them. My three quartets would certainly not have been possible without the Ardittis. It is not only a matter of unique brilliance of technique but also of passionate and touching musicality which moves me in certain phrases, certain shifts of fingering and colour-intensity more than I can say.

How do you see the prospects for music at the end of the century?

I find it quite difficult to comment on the immense plurality of our time and what is good and what is bad in this amazing mix of activity. What is clear is that anybody who seems to be very individual and separate and uninfluenced by anything else is really choosing an interiority quite *deliberately*, because the ease with which compact discs and broadcasts are disseminated and the ease of travel all make for great communicability of this mass of different ways of thinking.

So whether something is good or bad does not really depend on whether it is tonal or atonal or electronic or has had a brush with spectralism or not, although many of these things appeal to me personally in one direction rather than another. I think that is not the essence of the problem, or of the question, let us say. What I seek is music that is as fresh as an improvisation and yet has not a sound out of place. It is music that has a certain freedom. That is important, both sociologically and ethically and musically.

Another dimension of this question is that I like to hear music which is creating a kind of integration between the linear music of past centuries and the global music that has characterized our own century. These types of music are really about different times, thinking about time in a different way. As I said before, linear music is concerned with composing against what has happened already, what has been established as a pattern, so that is a vivid force in the now, in the present. The now is always informed by a tension against what has just happened, a breaking up of what has just happened and breaking out of it in some way, either by violent contrast or by slight contrast or by near similarity or by exact repetition. It all makes a meaningful interval and a meaningful statement with its own colour and tension.

The other type is to do with eternity; it is more to do with spirituality, it is more to do with seeing everything as a whole, as a unity, from above, and it doesn't have the tension of the detail. As I was saying with the Goethe and Steiner approach to a world view, we start with a general feeling for eternity and unity, we arrive at the specific individuality in detail, and that detail is informed and made more vivid by what was preliminary to it; whereas the current paradigm is to work from detail to a kind of abstraction – a law, which really reduces the detail ultimately to being less interesting than its explanation. This isn't real knowledge; it is knowledge about things, not knowledge of things in all their vividness.

So I think there has to be a marriage of both of these types of time, and that is the kind of music, regardless of its style or whatever, that I find the most interesting. And of course the more contrasts there are, the more violent the contrasts, the more difficulties that are unified, the more interesting the music. Ultimately this is a spiritual and ethical matter. Messages can't be avoided in music. Those who say that they are not interested in messages are really deluding themselves. Music is never value-free; even though it seems to be silent on things, those silences are significant – they add up to a statement. Therefore one has to take on board that music has a purpose and think about it and make sure that, as a composer, your music has the purpose you have thought carefully about.

So, what is the purpose of music? It is, in my view, to reveal the nature of suffering and to heal. The one big question of existence. And the nature of suffering is connected with the separation of self and other, the narrow ego which is set up as an illusory existent, the belief that I am separated and therefore in a relationship of duality and even of conflict with the world: even physical suffering is subtly connected with this. So these are things which music, as it were, represents a statement about. This is the purpose of music. Music can be cathartic in its great tragic moments; it can heal; it can bring together violent and unexpected contrasts in a way that is free and shocking and it can bring together music from different styles, tonal and atonal; it can bring together world musics from abrasively different cultures; it can bring together dance and music, film and music, sound and light; any of these conjunctions will more and more freely, I feel, become integrated in this basic purpose of music to somehow integrate and heal, heal things which seem necessarily individual and different.

As I said before, spectralism itself is a technique, a way of thinking about music which goes deeply into the stuff of music, the nature of music, so there is not very much room for any leftover, anything which isn't spectralism; ultimately spectralism is at the basis of music, it is the nature of sound; and sound, of course, we know is shaped to become various illusory forms, themes built of a few sound elements, and these few sound elements are rearranged to form another element of music which is at a higher level, like a melody or a motif, or a Beethoven symphony. But that, even so, can be extended to any medium of art. It is not just the nature of sound, it is the nature of light, it is the nature of colour, the nature of semantic meaning, the nature of drama. All these things can become part of the manifold representation of a rich and incredibly complex world which is ultimately at war with itself because it believes itself to be differentiated.

The last thing I would want would be a colourless, empty world, yet paradoxically – at a deeper level – that is the only thing I want, because without some notion of release from an illusory way of conceptual thought, how can we ever gain the peace, the tranquillity of mind, the clarity of vision which will enable us to see things as they truly are? In fact, these words are quite inadequate, the words of emptiness and lack of existence. From what I have experienced of such things, they are actually the opposite. They have more the feeling of being full, and yet it is not full in the way we normally mean the word. The feeling is of fullness; it is the opposite of the negative and it is only through the *via negativa* that one arrives at the state of true fullness.

So I don't want to look for anything else except purity of motive, as T.S. Eliot said, in what music of the future does; whenever it is based on such principles it will be good and true and important, and the message will be worth putting out. Composers' activities will be a part of civilization, a very important part of the evolution of mankind.

Commentary

Background and Beginnings

It is understandable that historians of music in the United Kingdom should regard 1934 as a year of particular significance. The year in which Elgar, Delius and Holst all died, in which Vaughan Williams, Tippett and Britten made important creative advances, and in which Maxwell Davies and Birtwistle were born, must surely lay claim to the embodiment of that decisive moment of transformation in which nineteenth-century values were finally laid to rest and a genuinely modern spirit came into proper prominence.

Such grand generalizations invariably collapse under more detailed scrutiny, and yet the sense of the mid-1930s as a critical dividing line retains considerable validity. For example, whereas those British composers born in the first half of the decade – pre-eminently Alexander Goehr, Peter Maxwell Davies and Harrison Birtwistle – developed their progressive approaches to style and structure in terms (broadly speaking) of traditional sound-sources and accepted (though far from inflexible) responses to established compositional genres and concepts of the musical work, those born between the mid-thirties and mid-forties seemed to benefit from a far more heterogeneous musical environment. Some, like Jonathan Harvey (born in 1939) have attached particular importance to electro-acoustic possibilities; some have reinforced the continuing attractions of allusions to tradition (Nicholas Maw, Robin Holloway); others have embraced the drastic rethinking of compositional character known as minimalism (Gavin Bryars, John Tavener), or have committed themselves to more complex textures and hyper-expressionistic moods (Brian Ferneyhough, Michael Finnissy). But no example from within this cast is more interesting than that of Harvey himself. By date of birth alone it would be appropriate if he were to represent a bridge between the 'old-style' avant-garde predispositions which have been worked out in very different ways by Goehr, Birtwistle and Maxwell Davies and the particular range of spiritually orientated, texturally elaborate possibilities which arise if one imagines (or tries to imagine!) a fusion of Tavener and Ferneyhough.

As Harvey's own comments on his early development in the interview included in this handbook make clear, he experienced to the full the extraordinary flowering – and potential confusions – of a time when interactions between national and international orientations were notably rich and complex. To study in England with Erwin Stein, to profit from contacts with Benjamin Britten and Hans Keller, to have church music traditions in one's blood: such contrasts and contradictions could be deeply inhibiting to personalities without strong creative impulses of their own. That Harvey had such impulses in abundance is apparent as early as the *Little Concerto for Strings*, composed in 1961, during his student years, and revived in 1997. This has the kind of modal harmonic rootedness which he would avoid in his later music: yet there is a rhythmic flow, and a sense of purposeful thematic evolution and growth, expressed through a confident handling of the chosen medium, that is mature and personal enough to explain why Harvey thought it worth resurrecting this score, with only slight changes, thirty-six years after it was composed.

What the *Little Concerto* confirms is that even in his earliest works Harvey was able to move beyond mere imitation of then-potent idioms – particularly, in England, the still relatively traditional music of Britten and Tippett. As he began to achieve some recognition as teacher and composer, Harvey was to distance himself more determinedly from such immediate and in many ways attractive models, making contact with some of the most radical creative – and didactic – spirits of the 1960s. By the early 1970s he was evidently more at ease with what he calls the 'dark and strong states of intense experience' of post-war European High Modernism – Boulez, Xenakis, Stockhausen – than were any of his slightly older English contemporaries, even though he shared with many of those contemporaries a feeling for what was most stimulating in the music of Olivier Messiaen. Harvey also experienced the trials and tribulations of increasing success and prominence at a time when he was still working his way towards his own particular stylistic and technical synthesis. The result was a group of quite substantial early works (culminating in *Persephone Dream* of 1972) which are more representative of an idiom in evolution than of a wholly personal voice. They are nevertheless important for laying appropriate foundations, and for providing the outlines of those qualities which the later works have explored more consistently and comprehensively.

From the 1960s to the 1970s

Pride of place among these early scores should go to the Symphony (1966). That this was originally thought of as *Three Pieces for Orchestra* might suggest that its symphonic status is at best ambivalent, and it is certainly unusual in the way that a relatively substantial first movement is followed by a terse scherzo, and then a slow finale which seems to make a point of shunning conventionally cumulative strategies. The first and second movements can be felt to represent Harvey's particular homage to his 'Viennese' teachers Stein and Keller, and the principal echoes to be heard in them range from Schoenberg, Berg and Webern to the then-recent *Little Symphony* (1963) by Alexander Goehr, itself a marvellously imaginative exploration of the possible conjunctions between Second-Viennese-School strategies and an essentially classical symphonism. But Harvey abandons this model in his finale, the Symphony's most striking and idiosyncratic movement, which has a ritualistic quality in its use of ostinatos and exploitation of registral extremes. Such a pared-down meditative music is an intriguing precursor for the most personal and powerful aspects of Harvey's mature music, but it was to be some time before he found a way to move it into the centre of his creative concerns.

Between the *Little Concerto* and the Symphony, Harvey had written a String Quartet (now withdrawn), reflecting 'Bartók, Tippett and Fauré' (as Bayan Northcott noted in *Grove*, 1980) and a *Triptych* showing 'an interest in Schoenbergian serialism and Messiaen's modal technique'. This early eclecticism was rounded out by works revealing Britten-like features (*Yeats Songs* and *Cantata I*), although the *Cantata* (1965) has a way with astringent choral harmony and expressionistic atmosphere, including choral *Sprechgesang*, that shows some affinity with Peter Maxwell Davies. After the Symphony it was to these more immediate avant-garde developments among his closer contemporaries that Harvey increasingly turned; in particular to Stockhausen (*Chaconne* for orchestra, 1967) and Maxwell Davies (*Cantata III*, 1968). Also from 1968, the *Transformations of 'Love bade me welcome'* for clarinet and piano can easily be aligned with memories of Messiaen and awareness of Maxwell Davies – especially his writing for Alan Hacker in *Hymnos* and other scores. But *Transformations* also provides evidence of Harvey's personal way of thinking about harmony. The beginning – a transcription of Harvey's setting of a poem by George Herbert (Ex.1) – is not tonal, and yet the chords are not exclusively dissonant. Rather, the traditional harmonic categories of relatively stable and unstable sonorities have been rethought, and the linear processes (voice-leading and rhythm) ensure an expressive profile that sets the scene for the strong contrasts of the variations which follow, and which display a fruitful, if not yet especially personal, response to the kind of alternations between expressionistic turbulence and lyric reflection that made Maxwell Davies's works of the 1960s (centring on the opera *Taverner*) so potent a presence on the British musical scene.

It was by way of large-scale texted compositions that Harvey was able to work through his own response to the varied issues apparent in sixties music – not least how to deal with the laudable desire of such well-established institutions as the Proms and the Three Choirs Festival to commission promising younger composers. At first glance, *Ludus Amoris*, a forty-minute cantata for the 1968 Three Choirs Festival, is significant primarily for its vivid treatment of the kind of spiritual topics that Harvey would make his own in the years ahead, but its very heterogeneity was a cause

EX. I. *Transformations of 'Love bade me welcome.'*

of concern to Bayan Northcott who, in the first extended study of Harvey's music, discussed its attempt 'to fuse visionary, symbolic, dramatic, verbal and musical layers of significance all at once on the largest scale'. A wide variety of texts is matched by music evoking Maxwell Davies, big-band jazz, Messiaen and Tippett, and Northcott was particularly unhappy about 'one passage of elaborately disorganised choral slogan-shouting' in which 'Harvey succumbs . . . to the naturalistic fallacy that vitiates so much contemporary art; a representation of chaos, not by careful slanting of expected musical procedures but by straight simulation' (Northcott 1973: 36).

Harvey's compositions of this period can certainly be seen as reflections of the particular difficulties of composing coherently and personally at a time when so many diverse and potent possibilities were there to be explored, the idea of single-minded progress and advance having definitively broken down. From a present-day perspective it is easy enough to hear how a work like *Benedictus* for orchestra (1970) conforms to the favoured contemporary plot of confrontation between a simple source (in the case of *Benedictus*, a nursery song, 'The farmer's in the dell') and expressionistic transformations of that source which, in effect, take the music to the opposite extremes of complexity and intensity. Writing when the piece was new, Northcott was uneasy with the 'subverted continuity' of such a formal procedure. Yet it is fascinating today to see how resourcefully Harvey reacted against the more connected style of his own earlier symphonic music, and in the Symphony and *Benedictus*, in particular, there are passages of relatively transparent texture and flexible construction in which the characteristic Harvey of the not-too-distant future can be seen in embryo.

One of the most successful pieces in its charting of a continuum of expressive and technical contrasts is the Piano Trio (1971). Sounding in some ways like a sketch for important aspects of the soon-to-be-written *Inner Light* trilogy, its three movements – 'Song', 'System', 'Rite' – move from the kind of melodic lyricism that Harvey would later identify with a blissful alleviation of suffering to a ritual that is wild in its fractured, aleatoric expressionism, and seems to represent the dark side of experience. (Ex. 2 shows the work's first, *cantabile* string phrase against its delicately patterned piano accompaniment.) While in later works Harvey has often, and understandably, preferred a progression from the darkness of expressionism to the light of ecstatically flowering melody, it is important to note that he has never suppressed the musical representation of this dark side. His music thrives, and has grown to its full maturity, by means of a dialogue between dark and light, suffering and healing, and not from the 'victory' of one over the other.

EX. 2. Piano Trio

High Modernism, and After

Given the vital role of electro-acoustic techniques in the development of Harvey's mature musical personality, it should be noted that it was in the same year as the Piano Trio, 1971, in *Cantata VII*, 'On vision', that he not only developed serial techniques further (having worked with Babbitt at Princeton during 1969–70) but also included an important part for tape. For the moment, however, he remained intensely involved with traditional instrumental, vocal and orchestral forces, and between 1971 and 1976 he was engaged in what now seems like an epic struggle to project his emerging philosophical and spiritual concerns through essentially expressionistic musical structures and gestures. The result was music of at times disconcerting density and stress, in which lyricism has to struggle to survive.

The orchestral symphonic poem *Persephone Dream* (1972) is certainly more assured than the Symphony or *Benedictus* in its formal control, the sense of an integrated process unfolding inexorably and with a strong expressive charge sustained consistently throughout. Harvey referred to 'several years of thought about the Eleusinian mysteries, Mediterranean light and landscape, and about Persephone, who descends from the flowery meadow to the dark regions of death, and then re-emerges joyfully to see her mother again' (Harvey 1973: 58). Musically, the work is part of his 'quest to rediscover structural depth' – a feeling for harmony operating on different structural levels – yet this quest 'has not deterred me from the use of a dramatic and expressionistic surface'. The main result of this urge to combine integration with intensity is a textural density that reinforces the music's avoidance of perceptible harmonic hierarchies in favour of hyperactive webs of melodic strata whose fundamental restlessness and instability Harvey would gradually turn away from, if only to contextualize them in a more positive, purposeful light. For Northcott, in 1973, *Persephone Dream* was 'perhaps the most sophisticated score written by any of the British composers at present in their mid-thirties', and he commented that 'Harvey's way forward might now seem clear'. At the same time, Northcott diagnosed a potential problem in that (as with Maxwell Davies) the deployment of extra-musical references to heighten musical meaning can often have the opposite effect by dissolving purely compositional process.

If he were prepared to forgo the expressive and visionary adjuncts to his composing, which others besides himself share and communicate, in order to concentrate upon the more 'limited' quest for new modes of articulation, new effects to communicate directly the significance of his serial discourse, he might grow surprisingly. After all, a perfectly defined 'absolute' work is no less witness to the divine order than a cantata with a text telling you about it. (Northcott 1973: 40).

As will be evident, Harvey did not respond to this challenge by rejecting those 'expressive and visionary adjuncts': rather, he sought to bring expression, and vision, closer to those 'harmonic procedures that will genuinely function once more as the centre of musical discourse' – to equate the musical centre with the spiritual focus. This new phase of his work, beginning very much as Northcott's article was being written, is that which most directly reflects Harvey's interest in the spiritual philosophy of Rudolf Steiner (1861–1925). (See above, pp. 14–15, for Harvey's own account of this topic.)

Vision and Tension

The *Inner Light* trilogy, which Harvey composed between 1973 and 1977, counts as transitional between the relatively heterogeneous but increasingly expressionistic early works and the later scores, which centre on his work with electro-acoustics and computers, principally at IRCAM and Stanford. Musically speaking, the three compositions (written in the order 1, 3, 2) explore interrelations and transformations which lead from sounds prerecorded and manipulated on tape to the 'live' music. 'In the first work [for seven instruments and tape] the tape is used to transform, by subtle inner changes, instrumental timbre to structural harmony; in the second [chamber orchestra with voices and tape] vowel sounds to harmony and instrumental timbre; and in the third [full orchestra and tape] one instrumental timbre into another.' In one sense, therefore, the trilogy is a 'sort of homage to Rudolf Steiner', and the idea of 'the expansion of the consciousness towards God'. Yet that process of expansion is mirrored in those timbral transformations which are the most explicit result of Harvey's work with electro-acoustics:

we have in timbre a concept that disappears into other things at the computer terminal but which reappears in an indefinable way in aesthetic experience. Since research into acoustics is one of the most exciting obsessions in music at present and probably in the future, this particular interchange between reason and soul is highly illuminating, and brings the 'indefinable' into ever sharper definition. As Rudolf Steiner believed, man's endeavour should ever be to make things more conscious. That is spiritual development. (Harvey 1986b: 179).

Writing of *Inner Light (3)*, Harvey explicitly associated his representation of a spiritual quest ('expansion of the consciousness towards God') with a musical quest for 'structural depth (in the Schenker tradition, maybe)', meaning that 'several levels of structure are inextricably woven together in a "nest", ranging from all the details and embellishment at the top to the single macrocosmic idea at the bottom' (Harvey 1976: 125). As our interview makes clear, however, Harvey was nevertheless well aware of the paradox of striving to embody the kind of integration which Schenker found only in classical tonal structures with his (Harvey's) contemporary, post-tonal concern for that 'timbral experience' which is, essentially, a matter of 'shifting identities', and the kind of timbral composition that plays with 'the identity given to objects by virtue of their having a timbre, in order to create *ambiguity*' (Harvey 1986b: 178-9). Certainly, in comparison with the works which were written in the years after *Inner Light*, the trilogy itself – and especially the third piece – seems more the apotheosis of an essentially expressionistic idiom than the dawning of a new style. Like *Perse-*

phone Dream, Inner Light (3) now seems relatively congested in texture and earnest in manner, despite the use of the kind of symmetrical sets that were to underpin Harvey's later harmonic thinking, and the powerful resonance of the material on tape. Both works tend more to evoke a 'seething world' of 'chaotic violence' than to reject it – or, more positively, they confront that world in order to exorcise it. But – particularly in *Inner Light (3)* – Harvey appears to be filling the available sound-space in order to counter any inherent hierarchic tendencies in his material, and the result is far less easy to align with fundamental humanizing genres of song and dance than most of Harvey's later works. From this perspective, it was only after the *Inner Light* trilogy that light and, with it, a fully achieved clarity and technical control, entered Harvey's music. Even so, clear pointers can be found – in the culminating vocal melody of *Inner Light (2)* (Ex.3), or the aspiring lyric ethos as song emerges from speech in the associated Steiner setting *Spirit Music* (1975) – to the kind of more contemplative yet far from exclusively other-worldly atmosphere of Harvey's more recent music; a music in which, as he puts it himself, he 'began to loosen up'.

The Resonance of Melody

In Harvey's mature post-tonal world, the world his music has inhabited since the mid-1970s, the best way to communicate some sense of structural depth is by composing clearly perceptible continuities between an initial, fundamental timbral-structural entity and those elaborations on and around it which may render its continuing significance doubtful, but which, in the end, can be felt to be constrained by its persistent, recurrent presence and influence. At the heart of Harvey's mature musical thinking is the perception that a single sound is at the same time a resonant acoustic complex, and that such resonance can promote both 'spectral' and spiritual exploration: spectral in the sense of technical workings inside sound itself, spiritual in the way that such workings can serve the purpose of an expression which aspires to the numinous, the transcendent. In the two great 'founding fathers' of twentieth-

EX. 3. *Inner Light (2)*: vibraphone and piano are ring modulated

century music, Schoenberg and Stravinsky, the capacity of radically progressive music to continue to explore archetypal states of
feeling and thought is fully revealed, and much in their most important compositions can be described in terms of the categories
Nietzsche associated with Greek tragedy: the cool constraints of
Apollo confronting the turbulent abandon of Dionysus, or – alter-
natively – of the no less potent confrontation between death
(Thanatos) and love (Eros).

Combining the calculations of technology with the rituals of religious observation might seem to imply a well-nigh exclusive emphasis on Apollonian virtues, and such an emphasis would indeed

EX. 3 (cont.). *Inner Light (2)*

represent a retreat from the confrontations and tensions with which both Schoenberg and Stravinsky, in their very different ways, were concerned. A generation after them, Messiaen's great achievement was to show how the Dionysian spirit could be brought within the framework of ecstatic spirituality without thereby losing all its physical, sexual energy, or its reliance on progressive compositional thinking, even if the darker, tragic spirit of incipient chaos was not preserved. Among Messiaen's pupils and successors, the balance between ecstatic ritual and tragic enactment has been explored in many different ways, with (it might be argued) only Xenakis displaying a true affinity with the elemental tensions of Greek tragedy itself. Stockhausen's psycho-dramas, from *Momente* and *Inori* to the operatic cycle *Licht*, have moved in very different directions in their concern with the relationship between the individual and the universal, and, while Harvey has more in common with Stockhausen's ideas about drama in music and the overriding importance of the will to transcendence than with naturalistic types of operatic subject, he has not lost all concern with the more immediately human predicaments – in particular, the suffering – on which properly tragic expression depends. To a greater extent than either his minimalist or complexist contemporaries, Harvey has continued to employ types of lyric expression whose stylistic and rhetorical resonances not only make his music more accessible, but also ensure that the pursuit of transcendental rituals is complemented by a persistent human presence. It was this presence that had to struggle to make itself heard in the major works before 1977.

New Clarity: from Winchester to IRCAM

The new clarity of Harvey's language, coupled with a new sense of 'structural depth' as involving a more explicitly hierarchic harmonic context and a more spontaneous melodic character, can be found in his first acknowledged string quartet (1977), whose initial, focal D motivates and controls the entire work. (Ex.4 juxtaposes the beginning and the end, a distance in time of about fifteen

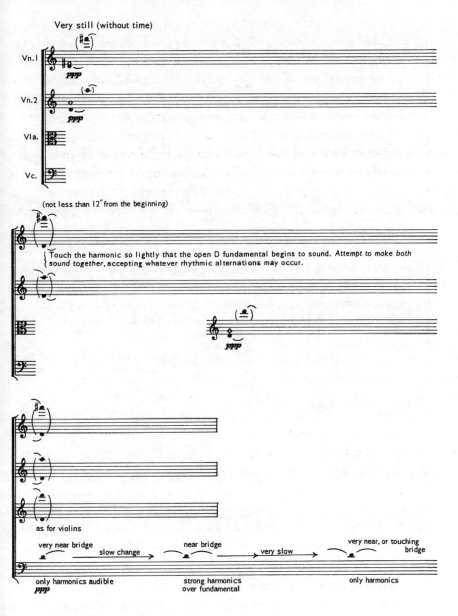

EX. 4A. String quartet [No. 1]

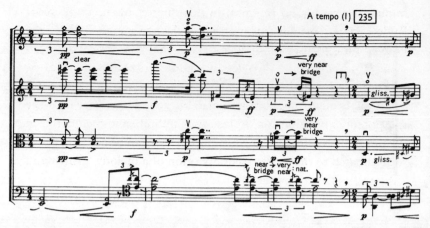

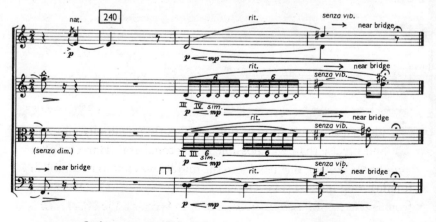

EX. 4B. String quartet [No. 1]

minutes.) There is no rejection in this quartet of the thinking of Rudolf Steiner, primary inspiration for the *Inner Light* trilogy. But Harvey now focuses on Steiner's claim that 'the future development of music will . . . involve a recognition of the special character of the individual tone' (Harvey 1982: 3). That 'tone' is not a traditional tonal tonic, but it is a stable centre against which the still potent expressionistic explosions – embodied in the quartet in a series of increasingly aggressive outbursts – can be contained and subordinated to the more essential notion of a melody 'growing in wisdom', as the composer's note describes it.

The late 1970s and early 1980s were a watershed for Harvey, centring on what he describes as the 'high time' of his involvement with various events at Winchester Cathedral, and also, providing the perfect architectural and acoustic complement to that sublime edifice, his first experience of IRCAM. The church opera in twelve scenes, *Passion and Resurrection,* completed in 1981, is the largest composition of this period, and Harvey's most extensive exploration of Christian themes, touching as these inevitably do on those archetypal topics of human suffering and spiritual transcendence which, for this composer, are as crucial a presence in Eastern as in Western religious thinking. The opera is also significant in providing the first example in his work (according to Harvey's recollection: see p. 17 above) of harmony which radiates outwards from a central axis of symmetry, providing the motivation for the composer's most striking (and easily misinterpreted) pronouncement: 'the bass moves into the middle: this is our musical revolution' (Harvey 1982: 2). This remark needs to be aligned with Harvey's earlier description of 'a musical language which is highly ordered, and yet which floats above the seething world of tonal becoming', providing 'a representation of this spirit world potentially more direct and precise than was possible in the tonal era' (Harvey 1980: 699–700). Moving the 'bass' into the middle was not to re-establish tonality, and often, as in a simple example of symmetrical inversion from Scene 12 of *Passion and Resurrection* (Ex. 5), the effect is of a bass-less contrapuntal music of equal voices, where the focal axis of symmetry may not be literally present, or not strongly asserted.

53

SCENE 12: THE RESURRECTION GARDEN:
The three Marys enter in the dawning light, singing as they come.

EX. 5. *Passion and Resurrection*

Harvey also says of the church opera that he 'found music for the first part, 'Passion', which was rather austere, quite cruel and brutal' (p. 17). The purely instrumental passage depicting the 'Anguish and Despair of Jesus' (whose ending is shown in Ex.6) certainly has some of that seething angularity familiar from Harvey's earlier, more orthodoxly expressionistic textures, not least that of *Inner Light (3)*. The overall character of the opera is nevertheless more in keeping with a tradition whose most recent developments had been provided by Britten's Parables for Church Performance of the 1960s (*Curlew River*, *The Burning Fiery Furnace*, and *The Prodigal Son*), and Harvey indicates not only that the 'musical fabric' of the work derives from two plainsong hymns – 'Sing my Soul' and 'The Royal Banners', but that, as in Britten's *St Nicolas* and *Noye's Fludde*, the 'audience or congregation' may participate in the singing.

Two years before completing *Passion and Resurrection* Harvey had written a substantial work for Winchester Cathedral's 900th anniversary which takes a familiar hymn tune – Parry's 'Laudate Dominum' – as its starting point. Parry's tune for 'O praise ye the Lord' is often remembered for the curious way its setting of the hymn's second line – 'praise him in the height' – descends to the depths, and there is undoubtedly something almost comic in the blithe muscularity of its celebratory tone.

Harvey's *Hymn* (1979) begins with a 'straight' arrangement of the first verse for choir and orchestra, to be performed 'with extreme cheerfulness'. With the second verse the process of change begins, and while Harvey's purpose is not a disconcerting deconstruction of an 'innocent' musical object of the kind Alfred Schnittke visits on Gruber's 'Silent Night' (*Stille Nacht*, for violin and piano), the transformation of uncomplicated communal praise into modern, and musical questing prayer (by way of the explicit verbal link between 'praise' and 'pray') is uncompromising enough to recall the earlier example in his work of an artless tune diffused into a radically 'other' musical world, in *Benedictus*. With the abandonment of the hymn text for words from the *Song of Solomon* which celebrate the power of love, both human and di-

EX. 6. Passion and Resurrection

vine, the spiritual pilgrimage embodied in the music is reinforced, and one of Harvey's most appealing and intriguing scores moves to its end.

Two other works from 1979 inhabit related regions. *Concelebration*, for flute, clarinet, cello, percussion and piano, is dedicated to the then Bishop of Winchester, and the specific spiritual image of a joint celebration of Mass underpins music in which elements still close to expressionistic turbulence acquire a meditative, ecstatic sheen anticipating the instrumental character of *Bhakti* (1982). *Be(com)ing* for clarinet and piano offers an even more intense exploration of ecstatic expressionism, and also demonstrates that voracious appetite for exploring new or recently developed possibilities in instrumental sound – for both clarinet and piano – which was the prime motivation for Harvey's persistence in working with electronics, and which entered a newly productive phase after his first contacts with IRCAM.

Technology and Transcendence

Earlier in this volume Harvey speaks of his experiences at IRCAM, not least in connection with *Mortuos plango, vivos voco* for eight-channel tape (1980), which manages to be both a technical exercise and a marvellously moving, allusive work – the great tenor bell of Winchester and the treble voice of his son Dominic providing the source material for a first, nine-minute attempt at timbral composition using the then-latest technology. Here is the definitive evidence of Harvey's ability to avoid succumbing to the purely technical ethos of electro-acoustic routines, and the composer's description of the piece reinforces those essential modernist aesthetic attributes of ambiguity and multiplicity which are no less relevant here than to his compositions involving 'live' instruments and voices: 'the aim of the piece might be described as coaxing us to hear abnormally, to hear a spectrum as de-fused individualities. Or rather, the aim is to hear it *both* that way, and the normal way, simultaneously' (Harvey 1986b: 181). Not only do these two ways of hearing interact, therefore: they are interdependent, and *Mor-*

tuos plango, vivos voco would indeed be in danger of seeming a mere technical exercise if they were not.

In *Bhakti* for chamber ensemble and quadraphonic tape – Harvey's second IRCAM composition, and completed in 1982 – techniques comparable to those employed in *Mortuos plango* achieve an even richer deployment, along with the explicit adoption of that symmetric, 'bass-in-the-centre' approach to harmony mentioned above. Harvey's note in the score declares that 'the musical syntax is symmetrical around a central axis. The ear is unconsciously attracted to hear the harmony not as dissonant over a fundamental bass but as floating free from bass functions yet rigorously controlled'. In our interview, he comments particularly on aspects of the ninth movement (shown in part in Ex. 7), whose stark simplicity, as a sonic response to the vastness of space to which the inscription at the end alludes, represents the furthest extreme from that 'seething expressionism' to which I've referred in connection with various earlier works. But the printed score cannot convey the richness of resonance which emanates from the interaction between the multiple octave Gs on the tape and the Gs sounded by the 'live' instruments. What the composer describes as 'an elaborate three-minute movement of spectral exploration' also embraces the stark contrast between the sustained Gs and the brief but explosive clusters shown in the tape part as dense black blocks – an indication, perhaps, that space is not simply awesome as the object of spiritual contemplation, but unpredictable, unknowable – at least without that 'transcendent consciousness' of which the composer also speaks.

'Bhakti' is a Hindu religious term, signifying devotion to a god, as a path to salvation. It is also a form of yoga, and its musical implications are most obviously to do with devotional states which combine the contemplative and the celebratory. Harvey makes these most explicit in quotations from the Sanskrit *Rig Veda* hymns which he places at the end of each of the work's twelve movements. Harvey links these to his Steinerian preoccupations with the claim that the inscriptions 'are keys to a transcendent consciousness', and the power of the music is undeniably the

EX. 7. *Bhakti*

(The quarters of the sky live on the oceans that flow out of her in all directions. The whole universe exists through the undying syllable that flows from her.)   *1.164*

greater for the sense (as if in acceptance of Northcott's argument) that no extra-musical heterogeneity is present to dilute the synthesis between musical strategies and spiritual expression. In *Bhakti* the music transforms its spiritual and structural unity into a compellingly coherent diversity of well-contrasted lyric and dramatic forms, and it culminates in the kind of exuberantly flowering melody – a song/dance synthesis – that will feature in many works from now on. And yet although, as Harvey has observed, 'my aesthetic predilection is to integrate ever more and more; through seamless transitions timbres are integrated with the structure and . . . structure is integrated with timbre' (1986b:180), the modernist disjunctions of the contemporary style cannot be denied. Speaking in the same context of the third movement of his *Song Offerings* (1985), to be discussed a little later, Harvey says that 'the whole movement, whose idea is that of mystical union, constantly moves in and out of fusion and fission. Is an instrumental part only a part or a thing in itself? Such is the ambiguity, the teasing veil of identity' (1986b: 181). As Harvey underlines, 'my work at IRCAM since *Mortuos plango* and *Bhakti* has been concerned with completely recognizable sounds and the paradox of their interchangeability. The aesthetic urge towards integration without losing individuality is my motive' (185): and yet, in those later works, as in *Bhakti*, 'ambiguity is constantly present in that the ear is often unsure whether it is hearing tape or live player' (184). Just as the ear 'modulates' between live and recorded, moving along the rich continuum which electro-acoustic techniques provide to connect different sounds, so the mind traces different paths through the nexus of spiritual and secular associations which the music can create.

Imaginary Rites

Bhakti can stand as a defining moment in Harvey's development, and despite the evidence it provided for the particular rewards of combining electro-acoustic and live sound, it did not lead to any narrowing-down in the areas of his compositional activity. Not only did Harvey continue to write works with no electronic dimension, but he made no attempt to close off associations with various aspects of tradition.

This diversity can be connected to some extent with the variety of institutions with which Harvey has been associated. At IRCAM he has been able to explore particular technical possibilities over extended periods, and the two works composed there after *Bhakti* – *Ritual Melodies* (conceived in 1985, completed in 1990) and *Advaya* (1994) – demonstrate his compositional thinking at its most visionary and probing. In *Ritual Melodies*, for quadraphonic tape, the ability of 'sounds generated artificially by computer', which are the piece's sole material, to intermodulate – to establish individual identities and at the same time to transform themselves into each other – required, as Harvey has indicated in notes with the CD recording, 'a revolution in programming', which was achieved with the help of Jan Vandenheede. No more than with *Mortuos plango, vivos voco* or *Bhakti* is the result an abstract technical exercise, however, and Harvey describes *Ritual Melodies* as 'an imaginary rite' whose use of sounds evoking 'Indian oboe, Vietnamese koto, shakuhachi, Tibetan temple bell, Western plainchant voice and Tibetan chant voice' reinforces the profound connections so many of Harvey's later works establish between the evolution and interaction of melodic strata and the creation of a meditative atmosphere within which dialogues between the generic attributes of devotion (melody) and ecstasy (dance) can unfold. As Harvey's comments in our interview make clear, the material of *Ritual Melodies* is a chain of differently 'coloured' melodies which evolve in an 'endless' loop away from and back to the original shape. Ex. 8 shows the beginnings of five of the lines (for the complete set, and an exhaustive analysis, see Vandenheede 1992), and indicates the simple, background (G-centred) modality as well as the more florid decorative – ritualistic – gestures from which the entire fabric is woven.

Ritual Melodies is a formidably convincing demonstration of how complex technical concerns can promote engaging expressive ends, yet *Advaya* is even more representative of its composer in the

EX. 8. *Ritual Melodies*

sense that it is not 'purely' electronic, but embeds the 'live' instrument in a complex electro-acoustic network of transformational technology. This is a work that 'needs a total of 2 players and 2 or 3 technicians for the electronics', whose elements consist of 'a set of floppy disks for the sampler and 2 CDs'. The intention is to dramatize the Buddhist concept of 'Advaya', the aspiration to transcend duality without denying its existence altogether. One can see here the practical consequences of Harvey's confession that

> *the aesthetic urge towards integration without losing individuality is my motive . . . It is important because art is a means of expanding the tight ego to the larger, more compassionate one, or to the 'egoless-ness' of Buddhism. Art's function is essentially ethical, ultimately spiritual. Any new consciousness born through experiencing, for instance, a timbral transition is a step in this direction, a life changed. (Harvey 1986b: 186-7).*

The very elementary – elemental – musical premises and timbral transitions of *Advaya* are direct evidence of the power which this uncompromising vision exercises over Harvey's creative work. As he says, 'the two players on stage both play only cello-derived sounds: live and electronic sound are one world, and much of the piece comes from transformations of one cello sound, that of the open A'. Here, even more than in other recent compositions, Harvey's remark that 'to achieve a frisson of richness it is always necessary to impose rigorous limitations' (1986b: 183) is of the essence: and yet the artistic necessity of ambiguity is not excluded. As with the third movement of *Song Offerings*, the music 'constantly moves in and out of fusion and fission. Is an instrumental part only a part or a thing in itself? Such is the ambiguity, the teasing veil of identity' (1986b: 181). (The text of *Song Offerings* at the point to which Harvey refers is 'in the perfect union of two'). As for *Advaya*, it is the best example to date of his concern to use the studio environment in general, and IRCAM in particular, as a location for meditative retreat, a source of sustenance from which music of particularly intense exploratory vision can emerge.

From the '80s to the '90s

After the twin peaks of *Passion and Resurrection* and *Bhakti*, Harvey advanced into the 1980s with a series of compositions notable for their flexibility and imagination. The material and ethos of the church opera continued to reverberate – literally in *Easter Orisons*, written for the Northern Sinfonia in 1983, with its striking dialectic between the earthbound and the ethereal. Exploration of instrumental sound without the aid of electronic manipulation continued in *Curve with Plateaux* (1982), a composition for solo cello which foreshadows *Advaya* in the way it works intensively with reiterated notes, curving away from and back to a low D while allowing the melodic phrases to flower with an immense variety of ornamental devices, so that the whole piece projects a kind of ritual melody.

In three further compositions for chamber ensemble or chamber orchestra – *Gong-Ring* (1984), *Tendril* (1987) and *Valley of Aosta* (1988) – Harvey approached a variety of challenges in ways which

63

made clear that *Bhakti* had not led to fixed ideas about instrumental structures. *Gong-Ring* involves electronics (ring modulation), and the result is a brilliant kaleidoscope, demanding considerable virtuosity, both individually and collectively. *Tendril*, a vivid response to a line by e. e. cummings – 'luminous tendril of Celestial wish' – uses just eleven players, including single strings and no percussion, while *Valley of Aosta*, for thirteen players, goes to the opposite extreme to the extent that its four wind and four string players are balanced by percussion, two harps, piano, two synthesizers (one player) and computer sequencer. The imaginative and dramatic power of this music perhaps indicates its position as a piece composed in the 'aftermath' of Harvey's most substantial enterprise of the mid-eighties, *Madonna of Winter and Spring* for full orchestra, synthesizers and electronics (to be discussed below), and although, as the title suggests, the work is on one level a response to Turner's majestic landscape of 1836 – 'Valley of Aosta: Snowstorm, Avalanche and Thunderstorm' – it is also, as the composer's note in the score explains, the product of the 'cultural perspectives' consequent on his receiving an important commission from a French ensemble, L'Itinéraire. The transcendence of opposition is again the essential concept, and Harvey speaks in the score of a music which

dissolves subject-object duality as idea and colour unite, and thematicism melts into psychic flow. Such a music could represent an ideal consciousness released from pragya pradh – the 'mistake of the intellect', wherein the intellect discriminates between objects so obsessively it forgets they are only given structure by the intellect itself.

On one level, then, *Valley of Aosta* is analogous to Turner's painting: 'it has no discernible figures or objects; it is an explosion of energy and diffracted light', and the harmony 'is not stated by sustained lines but by short points of sound; it is atomized, pulverized, with light shining through', a state in which the contribution of the 'computer-driven sequences for the synthesizers' is crucial. On another level, no less palpable, the music aspires to the spiri-

tual state of 'an ideal consciousness' in which the allusion to a natural landscape of awe-inspiring power is swept up into an irre-
sistible 'psychic flow', transcending 'avalanche and thunderstorm'
even as these forces of nature are most powerfully evoked.

Texts and Transformations

The progression from representation of the world of nature to a
more determinedly mystical vision of worlds beyond is charted in a
work for soprano, piano and tape from 1984. *Nachtlied* begins
with a setting of one of the most famous of all poetic evocations of
nocturnal serenity, Goethe's 'Wanderers Nachtlied' – a song which,
through Schubert's setting, is also emblematic of the special abilities
of musical romanticism to suggest a harmony between man and nature in which questions about more explicitly spiritual dimensions
may be (if only temporarily) set aside. Goethe's sublime humanism
is complemented in *Nachtlied* by Rudolf Steiner's poem, 'Evening
Meditation/Morning Meditation', which speaks of leaving 'the
realms of the veils of Being' and of ascending 'into the Divine'. The
matching progression of the music is from the rapt contemplative-
ness with which the Goethe setting begins to the extraordinarily
flexible intensity – at times narrowly focused, at times highly ornamental – with which those 'realms of the veils of Being' are evoked.

One recurrent image in Harvey's later work (inspired by Buddhist thinking) is that of an Emptiness which is less to do with negative associations of absence and loss than with the attainment of
freedom from egocentric suffering, and with the dissolving of concrete, striving entities into a kind of blissful flux. Dedicated to the
composer/conductor James Wood, *Forms of Emptiness* for unaccompanied mixed choir (1986) explores this topic by way of skil-
fully managed conjunctions between poems by e. e. cummings and
words from the Heart Sutra. Later, in 1997, Harvey returned to
the image in another composition dedicated to James Wood –
Wheel of Emptiness for sixteen players. But the significance of this
concept is not confined to these two works: rather, its value for
Harvey is precisely in the profound and wide-ranging musical pos-

65

sibilities it suggests – not least where the choice of texts for setting, or as background material for compositions, is in question.

In Harvey's recent vocal music, the tendency in those earlier works up to and including *Inner Light (2)* to employ large amounts of text in a variety of presentations, from spoken to sung, is increasingly tempered by a concern to focus more intensively on spiritual moods and attitudes. A considerable range of vocal techniques continues to be called for, as *How could the soul not take flight* (1997), for the National Youth Choir of Great Britain, demonstrates. Nevertheless, it remains more difficult for vocal writing to match the aspirations to ecstasy and transcendence that instrumental lines (especially with electronic transformation) can convey. *Song Offerings* for soprano and eight instrumentalists (1985) achieves a particularly memorable culmination not in ecstatic elaboration but in the quiet presentation of a bride's passive acceptance as she comes to 'meet her Lord alone in the solitude of the night'. Taken literally, Tagore's poem might outrage contemporary feminist sensibilities, but as a metaphor for the human soul's necessary submissiveness, as it opens itself to the prospect of divine illumination, it presents a powerful and persuasive image – one which Harvey's restrained yet rapt vocal line matches perfectly (Ex.9). In contrast, the possibility that dance-like vocal exuberance can risk seeming effortful is shown earlier in *Song Offerings*, and also in the slightly later *From Silence* (1988), where there is an even greater contrast between the human strivings of vocal melody and the ability of electro-acoustic transformation to evoke the 'transcendental immensity of starspace' (as Harvey puts it in his notes with the recording) and to suggest an overwhelming flow of spiritual energy. It seems almost inevitable, therefore, that in *From Silence*, with its concluding hymn to the all-embracing power of Christ, the last 'word' should be unequivocally given to the mystical voice of electro-acoustic sounds. (See Harvey's comments on this work in the interview above, p.30.)

EX. 9. *Song Offerings*

EX. 9 (cont.). *Song Offerings*

Madonna of Winter and Spring

With works like these, which concentrate on devotional states and aspirations to transcendence, and which have little or nothing of the dark side of human experience, the suffering and pain of so much contemporary secular consciousness, Harvey is obviously at his furthest remove from the concerns of liberal humanism and social-democratic aesthetics. Other, often larger works have a wider scope, and in the years immediately after *Bhakti* none is more memorable, or successful, than *Madonna of Winter and Spring*, Harvey's response to a BBC commission for the 1986 Proms.

To hear *Madonna* immediately after Harvey's earlier large-scale orchestral/electronic composition, *Inner Light (3)*, is to become vividly aware of the changes in his compositional thinking over the ten years which separate the two scores, especially in the matter of harmonic structuring. Gone is the tendency to congestion and strenuous complexity. This is emphatically not to say that the later work lacks tension or drama, but the conflicts expressed in its dancelike first section have more in common, rhythmically, with Tippett or Messiaen than with Stockhausen or Ferneyhough, and the harmony is far more open to the rich resonance of consonance, albeit deriving from symmetrical rather than rooted sonorities. The music charts an elemental progression from its initial 'Conflict' – one of Harvey's most brilliantly orchestrated dance-movements – through sections, marked 'Descent' and 'Depths', in which the dark side of experience is tellingly evoked, to a vision of Mary, the Mother of God, which is increasingly light-filled and ecstatic. At times, this music may even seem about to align itself with the much simpler and sweeter compositional vocabulary of a comparable yet wholly different musical mind, that of John Tavener. As a whole, however, *Madonna of Winter and Spring* is a very personal and individual triumph, not least as a demonstration of the structural and expressive potential inherent in that technique of thematic working, composing with a circular chain of melodic lines, that informs so many of Harvey's works at this time. As Harvey has put it, 'if melodies are both strongly themselves and also embed fragments of other melodies in themselves, then they have what I always seek, some degree of ambiguity, some degree of structural depth' (1986a: 431), and it is this association between ambiguity and 'depth' which ensures that Harvey's music never floats away into the absolute purity of the meditative contemplation of eternity – a region where art as such must surely become irrelevant, if not inconceivable.

Into the '90s

It is impossible for this relatively brief Commentary to mention, let alone discuss, all Harvey's compositions – even the more substantial ones. Since 1990 he has sustained the productivity of the 1980s, and has continued to develop his compositional voice with unflagging resource and discrimination.

The new decade was launched with a work – Cello Concerto – whose plain generic title is increasingly rare for Harvey, but this in no way signifies a retreat from his overriding concern with musical images of aspiration to the spiritual bliss that can transcend suffering. Harvey's writing for cello – the instrument he himself played a great deal in earlier years – has always displayed a special intensity, making enormous technical and emotional demands on the performer, and with Frances-Marie Uitti, for whom the concerto was designed, he found an ideal interpreter in emotional commitment and technique alike. The kind of 'vocal' odyssey that the evolution of a concerto for solo instrument and orchestra inevitably establishes has something dramatic – and potentially operatic – about it, so it is fitting that the years immediately after the Cello Concerto should have been the ones in which Harvey brought to fruition a very long-term operatic project.

Inquest of Love (completed in 1992) is a two-act, 135-minute work requiring thirteen solo singers, male chorus, orchestra and electronics (three synthesizers). Harvey has said (in the English National Opera programme book) that 'my first idea was a sound of the sort only electronics can produce. It was a long, static sound in which one could live; one could explore it like a space with one's ear, now listening to higher elements, now to lower: it seemed to be all around. What I have read and sensed about life after death seemed remarkably similar to living in this music, to being music', and so Harvey was led ('after about twenty-five years of noting down ideas') to draft a libretto concerned with the progression from life to life-after-death – 'a strange story of weddings, murders and the quest for understanding, healing and forgiveness in the afterlife'.

There was a particular difficulty in making those aspects of the drama dealing with 'real life' as immediate and persuasive as those taking place on a more purely spiritual plane, and, as Harvey admitted in his 1995 Bloch lectures at Berkeley, *In Quest of Spirit*, 'I found it extremely difficult to compose some of the music of suffering'. In the event, what Andrew Porter (*Observer*, 13 June 1993) categorized as 'the music of pain and despair' is particularly powerful and effective. Harvey commented that

David Rudkin, who helped make the libretto work for the theatre, urged me fully to face the consequences of what I had written, to descend completely into the katabasis of despair in order to evade nothing. I even composed a howl of pain – 'Why?' – in the text which the male protagonist screams out. It is sampled, looped and played back over and over, often very softly, so that the tissue of blending orchestral timbre can be woven out of the quality of pain.

Such despair is the dark night of the soul, from which the opera's principal characters eventually emerge into 'a new spirit of truth', to experience 'the peace that passes all understanding'. In these terms, Harvey's drama is not unlike a spiritualized version of Tippett's celebration of 'secular' psychology, *The Midsummer Marriage*, and the topics with which it deals reach into many of the composer's other works, written while the opera was being contemplated, and also in its aftermath. So, in the String Quartet No. 2 (1988) the music explores the interaction between melodic unanimity and its diffraction in ways which promote an ultimate dissolution of tension. In *Scena* for solo violin and ensemble (1992) a powerfully human sense of grief and rage (notably in the first section, marked 'Lament') leads, by way of an episode called 'Dream', to a 'Metamorphosis', an otherwordly sense of release. Similarly, *Lotuses* (also 1992) for flute (piccolo, bass flute), violin, viola and cello, charts a journey from a forceful, fiery opening to a gentle, delicate ending.

Lotuses also reflects, in a particularly telling way, the broader spiritual concerns that continue from *Bhakti* and extend the insights of Rudolf Steiner in the direction of Eastern religious philosophy and mysticism. Harvey has noted that 'in Buddhist writings the lotus, *padma*, signifies the world of form in all its individuality through which the light of reality shines. A lotus shows that individual objects, each one unique, are more enlightening to the awakening mind than abstract concepts'. The flexibility and directness evident in *Lotuses* is persuasive evidence of Harvey's ability to place his spiritual perceptions productively at the heart of his compositional practice. The result could hardly be less doctrinaire, and one need not share the composer's convictions – or even be aware of their existence – in order to respond to this highly refined and individual music, in which 'the world of form' achieves a potent reality.

After the two instrumental scores without electronics from 1992, and one from 1993 (*The Riot* for flute, bass clarinet and piano), Harvey returned to 'interactive' composition in two especially significant works completed in 1994. *Advaya* for solo cello, electronic keyboard and electronics has already been discussed in the context of Harvey's IRCAM projects, and the other piece also has a French connection. This is *Tombeau de Messiaen* for piano and digital audio tape, a memorial to the great French composer who died in 1992, music which in its rich chordal passages and hieratic dancelike episodes manages to evoke the master with no sense of slavish imitation. Moreover, although Messiaen himself had often exploited the subtle resonances of piano and metal percussion in combination, Harvey takes the resonant contextualizing of 'real' piano sound into a new dimension by shadowing it with a tape consisting 'of piano sounds tuned to twelve natural harmonic series'. As the notation in the score clearly indicates, the result – with the tape music shading in and out of 'well-tempered' tuning,

EX. 10. *Tombeau de Messiaen*

August 1994

73

but predominantly concerned to create a numinous aura around the live player – is a dialogue between two complementary versions of similar material, and a fine, very immediate demonstration of Harvey's favoured ambiguity, the two types of music both reinforcing and questioning the other as the work proceeds through a sequence of clearly patterned stages to a fierce climax and a rapid, stark descent, as if acknowledging the inescapable reality of death. (Ex. 10: for more on *Tombeau de Messiaen*, see p. 28 above.)

From Darkness to Light

The spiritual and aesthetic complement of *Tombeau de Messiaen* may be found in Harvey's first vocal work after *Inquest of Love*, *One Evening . . .*, for soprano, mezzo-soprano, chamber ensemble and electronics (also 1994). At thirty-four minutes, *One Evening . . .* is also the longest work from the 1990s after the opera, and the result of a particularly productive period of contact with York Höller and the Studio for Electronic Music in Cologne. This is one of Harvey's 'Eastern' works, with texts from Han Shan, Tagore and the Heart Sutra offsetting the anguished American words which Harvey describes in our interview, and although it can be placed in the long line of vocal compositions stemming from the early cantatas and on through *Inner Light (2)* to *Song Offerings* and *From Silence*, it achieves a new spontaneity and intensity. This is partly on account of the prominence and resourcefulness of the electronic element, the six 'conventional' instrumentalists balanced by five other performers – two playing the electronic keyboards, one operating the compact disc players and two technicians at the mixing desk – and partly the consequence of using two voices which can alternate and combine to create an atmosphere of remarkable sensuality as well as lyrical intensity.

In its expansiveness and dramatic scope, *One Evening . . .* could well be considered an epilogue to *Inquest of Love*. In turn, something of its atmosphere is carried over into *Soleil Noir/Chitra*, completed early in 1995, and scored for an ensemble of nine players, including synthesizer, and an electronic set-up controlled by two performers. The sense of a mystical, potent ritual is by now a familiar Harvey characteristic, but there is nothing routine in the way freshly imagined textures, full of light and space, devoid of any hint of oppressive density, are deployed in this substantial score. *Soleil Noir/Chitra* is also special in the nature of the associations implied by its title. On the one hand, 'soleil noir' is a phrase from a poem ('El Desdichado') by Gérard de Nerval – 'le soleil noir de la mélancholie' – which is the subject of an essay by the French psychoanalytic critic Julia Kristeva (see her *Soleil noir. Dépression et Mélancholie*, Paris 1987): on the other hand, *Chitra* is a poetic drama by Rabindranath Tagore derived from a story in the *Mahabharata*, about the marriage of the Princess Chitra to Prince Arjuna, a story of fulfilment in which the couple ultimately achieve what Arjuna calls 'that bare simplicity of truth'. Harvey is fascinated by the obvious and extreme contrasts between Kristeva's European Freudianism and Tagore's Asian spirituality – both, for him, equally profound and promoting a musical discourse of special intensity, which digs even deeper into the 'pain/bliss' dialectic than *One Evening* . . . (Ex.11 shows the evanescent ending of *Soleil Noir/Chitra* in the composer's MS.)

In the same year as *Soleil Noir/Chitra* Harvey completed two works without electronics. *Hidden Voice* (the title alludes to Baudelaire's 'L'invitation au voyage') is a short piece for chamber orchestra which initiated the composer's fruitful and ongoing association with Sinfonia 21, while the String Quartet No. 3 was written 'for the Arditti String Quartet in admiration', to a BBC commission. Here the principal effect is of a transformation of the ensemble's essentially lyrical persona by means of an immense variety of special playing techniques which inflect basic sounds through different tunings, harmonics, types of vibrato and playing positions, and even 'orchestrates' the breathing of the players at one point. Knowing of the composer's interest in electronics, it is impossible not to feel that the object is in some respects to evoke electronic transformation in its absence. Even so, there is no sense of awkward or forced distortions of 'proper' quartet style: rather, there is an imaginative extension of that style, and a subtly poetic transmutation of the genre's most fundamental attributes.

EX. 11. *Soleil Noir/Chitra*

EX. 11 (cont.). *Soleil Noir/Chitra*

Harvey also composed two choral works without electronics at this time, the *Missa Brevis* (1995), and *How could the soul not take flight* (1997), but his most striking recent use of this medium comes in *Ashes Dance Back* for a choir of at least twenty-eight singers and an electronic set-up including CD player, keyboard, digital samplers and effects processor. *Ashes Dance Back* was the first substantial work written in conjunction with the Center for Computer Research into Music and Acoustics at Stanford, and for his basic textual material Harvey turned to fragments of a text by Rumi, centring on images of rebirth and renewal. The score is prefaced with the following lines:

> *I burn away; laugh; my ashes are alive!*
> *I die a thousand times:*
> *My ashes dance back –*
> *A thousand new faces.*

Ashes Dance Back was written with the collective virtuosity of James Wood's New London Chamber Choir in mind, and its extensive use of phonetic exclamation, often in elaborate contrapuntal textures with a strong aleatory aspect, taps into a tradition of avant-garde choral composition that recalls the seminal example of Stockhausen's *Momente*. At the same time, however, Harvey's own propensity for more lyrical melodic elaboration is not suppressed, and – most striking of all – the work builds to a homophonic chorale-like texture before dispersing in a manner that suggests an ascent into transcendent delight rather than disintegration or dissolution.

Reference to the chorale as a generic icon occurs in other recent works, like the *Percussion Concerto* (1997) and *Calling Across Time* (1998). Of all Harvey's scores from the 1990s, the *Percussion Concerto*, written for Evelyn Glennie to perform at the Proms, might appear to be the most 'conventional', not simply because it requires no electronics (beyond an optional reverberation/amplification effect at the end) but because in the nature of the genre it is not possible to get 'inside' the sound, as Harvey puts it, as intensively as he is usually able to do. There are even hints of a Lutosławskian style in Harvey's textural layering – for example, the imitative brass fanfares at the very end. He nevertheless turns ostinato patterning and regular rhythmic figures into positive evolutionary elements, and the familiar generic attributes of song and dance are also significantly involved, giving the music an unambiguously personal slant.

Harvey in the late 1990s

Harvey has written eloquently of his feelings about the symbiotic relationship between the immediacy of human suffering and the rapt sublimity of spiritual aspirations to transcendence of all human experience and emotion. As already argued, it is in those works that emphasize the blissful prospect of such transcendence (*Ashes Dance Back* is one) that Harvey's music is most distant from the kind of 'mainstream' neo-expressionist idiom that embodies – often through a kind of vocal melody that expresses intense desolation and disorientation – a deeply human, unsparingly contemporary attitude. No composer has embodied this idiom more impressively than Harvey's exact contemporary Heinz Holliger, especially in his engagement with the poetry of Hölderlin, the very acme of a kind of Romantic agony that never bursts the bonds of purely poetic discipline and control. Holliger, acknowledging in particular the reticent lyric expressionism of Luigi Nono's late works, is able to demonstrate – as, in a very different manner, does Harrison Birtwistle in England – that a spirit of pessimism and bleakness can itself aspire to transcendence through the artistic power and vision, the affirming humanity, of its making: and (as noted earlier) Harvey, even with the very different emphasis that grows from his particular religious and aesthetic perspectives, has never excluded the dark side of experience, or the use of expressionistic elements, from his music. Nowhere, save perhaps in *Soleil Noir/Chitra*, is this aspect given more persuasive presentation than in *Death of Light/Light of Death* for oboe (cor anglais), harp/tam tam and string trio.

This work arose from a very special combination of circumstances.

Commissioned by the Musée d'Unterlinden, Colmar, for its 1998 Good Friday concert performed in front of Matthias Grünewald's 'Crucifixion' (the Isenheim Altarpiece), it also became a tribute to Harvey's father, Gerald Harvey, who died early in 1998, in his ninety-third year. It is organized into five movements, reflecting figures and events in the altarpiece – Jesus Crucified; Mary Magdalene; Mary, Mother of Jesus; John the Apostle; John the Baptist – and this sequence is striking in the obvious sense that it is not 'chronologically' conceived. Instead, the music progresses from the supreme crisis of the Crucifixion itself to the urgent hopefulness and unshakeable faith represented by John the Baptist. The effect is that, while dominated by images of lament – conveyed through searing instrumental writing which requires a wide range of oboe multiphonics, and with the other four instruments treated with all Harvey's characteristic technical resourcefulness – the climax is reached in processional music of an almost marchlike solemnity, signifying the determination and endurance of religious belief, and the conquering of death which this implies.

'Death constantly unweaves the thoughts that we have, in the course of our lives, so painstakingly woven together'. This is the first sentence of Harvey's note for a work written soon after *Death of Light/Light of Death*, and for an architectural setting very different from that of the Colmar Museum. *Calling Across Time* was commissioned by the British Library for performance at the opening of the new building on the Euston Road in June 1998, and although Harvey's note goes on to pay a graceful tribute to the way in which books, and the written word, can counter the corrosion of death and decay, his music, which is after all non-vocal, offers consolatory images of harmony and healing in purely musical terms. The 'calls' that are first heard, and which return towards the end, might on one level suggest growling Wagnerian dragons, but by the same token they stand for the positive, life-affirming power of musical memory, and the whole piece uses the image of memory and echo, most explicitly in the canonic exchanges between trumpet or harp and the electronic keyboard which can imitate them while projecting the imitation out into acoustic, architectural space. The effect is, ultimately, affirmative, and it is a measure of Harvey's increasing sympathy for 'spectral' harmonic processes that the rootedness of *Calling Across Time* should be ultimately suggestive of the most resonant of all musical memories in the 1990s – relatively stable consonance.

Provisional Conclusions

This commentary has traced developments and cross-currents in a creative odyssey spanning the best part of forty years. The diversity – at times, even the conflicts – within this substantial body of work are obvious; but in the end it is the continuity and the consistency which impress most deeply. Harvey's belief that music is 'the language of some greater consciousness', and that 'art's function is essentially ethical, ultimately spiritual' leads to the musical perception that melody is 'the bearer of feeling', and it is through the refinement and flexibility of his melodic writing, and its interaction with the no less essential harmonic dimension, that Harvey most memorably achieves the balance between tradition and innovation – and that 'certain freedom' – on which his music ultimately depends for its communicative power.

Complete List of Works

(published by Faber Music unless otherwise indicated)

Little Concerto for Strings (1961/97)
string orchestra
Duration: 10 minutes

Cantata I (1965) (pub. Novello)
soprano and baritone soli, SATB chorus,
organ and strings
Duration: 25 minutes

Four Songs of Yeats (1965)
(pub. Novello)
bass and piano
Duration: 9 minutes

Carol: 'Gaude Maria' (1965)
(pub. Novello)
bar. solo & SATB unaccompanied
Duration: 6 minutes

Variations (1965)
violin and piano
Duration: 13 minutes

Dialogue (1965)
cello and piano
Duration: 3 minutes

Symphony (1966)
(formerly *Three Pieces for Orchestra*)
Duration: 18 minutes

Cantata II – Three Lovescapes (1967)
(pub. Novello)
soprano and piano
Duration: 22 minutes

Iam Dulcis Amica (1967)
(pub. Novello)
SSATBB soli or choir
Duration: 7 minutes

Carol (1968) (pub. Novello)
SATB or AATB or TTBB unaccompanied
Duration: 9 minutes

Cantata III (1968) (pub. Novello)
soprano and 6 players
Duration: 25 minutes

*Transformations of 'Love Bade Me
Welcome'* (1968)
clarinet and piano
Duration: 11 minutes

In Memoriam (1969) (pub. Novello)
soprano, flute, clarinet, violin and
cello
Duration: 7 minutes

Cantata IV – Ludus Amoris (1969)
(pub. Novello)
soprano and tenor soli, speaker, large
SATB chorus and orchestra
Duration: 36 minutes

Four Images after Yeats (1969)
piano
Duration: 20 minutes

Laus Deo (1969)
organ
Duration: 4 minutes

Cantata V – Black Sonnet (1970)
(pub. Novello)
soprano, mezzo-soprano, baritone and
bass soli, and wind quintet
Duration: 8 minutes

Cantata VI – On Faith (1970)
(pub. Novello)
small SATB choir and small string
orchestra
Duration: 9 minutes

Benedictus (1970)
orchestra
Duration: 17 minutes

Studies (1970)
two equal clarinets
Duration: 13 minutes

Time-Points (1970)
magnetic tape (2-channel)

Trio (1971)
violin, cello and piano
Duration: 15 minutes

Cantata VII – On Vision (1972)
(pub. Novello)
soprano and tenor soli, large SATB
chorus and instrumental group
Duration: 26 minutes

Persephone Dream (1972)
orchestra
Duration: 16 minutes

Angel Eros (1973) (pub. Novello)
high voice and string quartet
Duration: 17 minutes

Inner Light 1 (1973)
7 players
Duration: 30 minutes

Quantumplation (1973)
flute, clarinet, violin, cello, percussion
and piano
Duration: 8 minutes

Round the Star and Back (1974)
(pub. Novello)
piano and a few other instruments
capable of a reasonable blend
Duration: 12 minutes

'The Dove Descending' (1975)
(pub. Novello)
SATB choir and organ
Duration: 5 minutes

Correspondences (1975) (pub. Novello)
mezzo-soprano and piano
Duration: variable – maximum 18 minutes

'Sobre un Extasis de Alta Contemplacion'
(1975) (pub. Novello)
SATB choir
Duration: 5 minutes

Cantata X – Spirit Music (1975)
(pub. Novello)
soprano, three clarinets and piano
Duration: 11 minutes

Inner Light 3 (1975)
orchestra
Duration: 32 minutes

'I Love the Lord' (1976) (pub. Novello)
SSAATTBB Choir
Duration: 4 minutes

'Song' (1977) (pub. Novello)
cello and piano
Duration: 3 minutes

Inner Light 2 (1977)
SSATB soli, instrumental ensemble and
tape
Duration: 36 minutes

Smiling Immortal (1977)
chamber ensemble of 11 players and
tape
Duration: 17 minutes

String Quartet No. 1 (1977)
Duration: 15 minutes

Magnificat & Nunc Dimittis (1978)
double SSATB chorus and organ
Duration: 12 minutes

Album (1978)
Seven miniatures for wind quintet
Duration: 18 minutes

Hymn (1979)
SATB chorus and orchestra
Duration: 21 minutes

Be(com)ing (1979)
clarinet and piano
Duration: 15 minutes

'O Jesu Nomen Dulce' (1979)
Motet for unaccompanied SATB chorus
Duration: 8 minutes

Concelebration (1979/81)
chamber ensemble of 5 players
Duration: 16 minutes

Resurrection (1980)
double SATB chorus and organ
Duration: 18 minutes

Toccata (1980)
organ and pre-recorded tape
Duration: 6 minutes

Mortuos Plango, Vivos Voco (1980)
computer-manipulated concrete sounds
(pre-recorded quadraphonic tape)
Duration: 9 minutes

Whom Ye Adore (1981)
orchestra
Duration: 15 minutes

Passion and Resurrection (1981)
Church opera in twelve scenes
Duration: 90 minutes

Modernsky Music (1981)
chamber ensemble of 4 players
Duration: 6 minutes

Bhakti (1982)
chamber ensemble and quadraphonic
tape
Duration: 50 minutes

Curve with Plateaux (1982)
solo cello
Duration: 12 minutes

Lullaby for the Unsleeping (1982)
medium voice and piano
Duration: 5 minutes

Nataraja (1983)
flute/piccolo and piano
Duration: 8 minutes

Easter Orisons (1983)
chamber orchestra
Duration: 19 minutes

The Path of Devotion (1983)
SATB chorus and small orchestra
Duration: 20 minutes

Flight Elegy (1983/89)
violin and piano
Duration: 9 minutes

Come Holy Ghost (1984)
unaccompanied double SATB chorus
Duration: 8 minutes

Nachtlied (1984)
soprano, piano and pre-recorded tape
Duration: 25 minutes

Gong-Ring (1984)
chamber ensemble and electronics
Duration: 22 minutes

Ricercare Una Melodia (1984)
trumpet and stereo tape-delay system
(version also with pre-recorded tape)
Duration: 6 minutes

Song Offerings (1985)
soprano and chamber ensemble of 8
players
Duration: 17 minutes

Madonna of Winter and Spring (1986)
orchestra, synthesizers and electronics
Duration: 37 minutes

Forms of Emptiness (1986)
unaccompanied SATB chorus
Duration: 13 minutes

God is Our Refuge (1986)
SATB chorus and organ
Duration: 5 minutes

Tendril (1987)
chamber ensemble of 11 players
Duration: 14 minutes

Lightness and Weight (1987)
tuba and orchestra
Duration: 14 minutes

Timepieces (1987)
orchestra (with two conductors)
Duration: 15 minutes

Lauds (1987)
SATB chorus and solo cello
Duration: 13 minutes

Valley of Aosta (1988)
chamber ensemble of 13 players
Duration: 14 minutes

From Silence (1988)
soprano, 6 players and tape
Duration: 21 minutes

String Quartet No. 2 (1988)
Duration: 16 minutes

Three Sketches (1989)
solo cello
Duration: 8 minutes

Thou Mastering Me God (1989)
SATB chorus and organ
Duration: 6 minutes

Ritual Melodies (1989–90)
quadraphonic tape
Duration: 14 minutes

Concerto for Cello (1990)
cello and orchestra
Duration: 19 minutes

'Praise Ye the Lord' (1990)
SATB chorus and organ
Duration: 4 minutes

Serenade (In Homage to Mozart) (1991)
wind ensemble of 10 players
Duration: 10 minutes

Fantasia (1991)
solo organ
Duration: 10 minutes

Inquest of Love (1991/92)
Opera in two acts
Duration: 135 minutes

Chant (1992)
solo viola
Duration: 3 minutes

Scena (1992)
violin and chamber ensemble of 9
players
Duration: 14 minutes

You (1992)
soprano and chamber ensemble of 4
players
Duration: 2 minutes

Lotuses (1992)

flute quartet
Duration: 17 minutes

Chant (1992/94)
solo cello
Duration: 3 minutes

The Riot (1993)
chamber ensemble of 3 players
Duration: 15 minutes

One Evening (1993–94)
soprano, mezzo soprano, chamber ensemble of 8 players, 2 technicians and
electronics
Duration: 35 minutes

Tombeau de Messiaen (1994)
piano and DAT tape
Duration: 9 minutes

The Angels (1994)
unaccompanied SATB chorus
Duration: 4 minutes

Advaya (1994)
solo cello, electronic keyboard and
electronics
Duration: 22 minutes

Pastorale (1994)
cello and harp
Duration: 3 minutes

Soleil Noir/Chitra (1994–95)
chamber ensemble of 9 players and
electronics
Duration: 15 minutes

Dum transisset sabbatum (1995)
Motet for unaccompanied SATB chorus
Duration: 4 minutes

String Quartet No. 3 (1995)
Duration: 16 minutes

Missa Brevis (1995)
SATB unaccompanied chorus
Duration: 10 minutes

Fanfare for Utopia (1995)
chamber orchestra
Duration: 1 minute

85

ff (1995)
solo piano
Duration: 2.5 minutes

How could the soul not take flight
(1996)
double unaccompanied SATB chorus
Duration: 15 minutes

Hidden Voice (1996)
chamber ensemble of 13 players
Duration: 7 minutes

Sufi Dance (1997)
solo guitar
Duration: 4 minutes

Wheel of Emptiness (1997)
chamber ensemble of 16 players
Duration: 16 minutes

Percussion Concerto (1997)
solo percussion and orchestra
Duration: 23 minutes

Ashes Dance Back (1997)
choir and electronics
Duration: 16 minutes

Still (1997)
tuba and electronics
Duration: 8 minutes

Haiku (1997)
solo piano
Duration: 1 minute

Calling Across Time (1998)
chamber ensemble
Duration: 16 minutes

Death of Light, Light of Death (1998)
chamber ensemble of 5 players after
Grunewald's Crucifixion in the
Issenheim Altarpiece
Duration: 17 minutes

*Homage to Cage, à Chopin (und Ligeti
ist auch dabei)* (1998)
piano and CD
Duration: 2 minutes

Tranquil Abiding (1998)
small orchestra
Duration: 14 minutes

Discography

Bhakti
Spectrum/Guy Protheroe
NMCD001

Bhakti
Nouvel Ensemble Moderne/Lorraine
Vaillancourt
Auvidis Montaigne MO 782086

**Cello Concerto* – Curve with Plateaux
– Ricercare una Melodia (cello) – Three
Sketches – Philia's Dream**
Frances Marie
Uitti/Orch.Sinf.dell'Emilia-Romagna
"Arturo Toscanini"*/Jose Ramon
Encinar*
Etcetera KTC 1148

Come Holy Ghost – I love the Lord
The Ionian Singers/Timothy Salter
Usk USK 1216CD

Come Holy Ghost – The Tree
Magdalen Oxford College Choir/
J Harper
Abbey CDCA915

**Come Holy Ghost – Carol – Forms of
Emptiness – I love the Lord – Lauds – O
Jesu Nomen Dulce – The Angels – Sobre
un extasis alte contemplacion – Two
Fragments**
Joyful Company of Singers/Paul Watkins
(cello)/Peter Broadbent
ASV CD DCA 917

Correspondences
Meriel Dickinson/Peter Dickinson
Unicorn Kanchana DKPCD9093

Dum transisset sabbatum
St Paul's Cathedral Choir/John Scott
Hyperion CDA66826

Fantasia
Kevin Bowyer
Nimbus NI 5509

From Silence – Nataraja – Ritual Melodies
Various/Karol Bennett/Barry
Vercoe/Harrie Starreveld/Rene Eckhardt
Bridge BCD 9031

God is Our Refuge
Choir of Chichester Cathedral/
Alan Thurlow
Priory PRCD 570

I love the Lord
Winchester Cathedral Choir/
Martin Neary
ASV CDQS6025

I love the Lord
Choir of King's College,
Cambridge/Stephen Cleobury
EMI CDC7 54418-2

I love the Lord
St Paul's Cathedral Choir/John Scott/
Andrew Lucas
Hyperion CDA66678

I love the Lord
New College Choir/Edward Higginbottom
Meridian CDE84123

I love the Lord
New College Choir/Edward Higginbottom
ProudSound PROUCD114

Imaginings
Frances-Marie Uitti/Jonathan Harvey
Chill Out CHILLCD007

**Lotuses – Scena – String Quartet No. 1 –
String Quartet No. 2**
Arditti Quartet/Felix Renggli

87

(flute)/Irvine Arditti (violin)/Nieuw
Ensemble/Ed Spanjaard
Auvidis MO 782034

Mortuos Plango, Vivos Voco
Erato 2292-45409-2

Mortuos Plango, Vivos Voco
Wergo WER2025-2

Serenade (In Homage to Mozart)
London PO/Andrew Parrott
EMI Classics CDC 7544242

Song Offerings
London Sinfonietta/George Benjamin
Nimbus NI 5167

String Quartet No. 1
Group for Contemporary Music
Koch 37121-2

Sufi Dance
David Starobin
Bridge Records 9084

The Tree
Norwich Cathedral Choir/Michael
Nicholas/N Taylor
Priory PRCD351

Valley of Aosta
Musique Nouvelle Ensemble/
Georges-Elie Octors
Ricercar RIC 07305

Bibliography

Writings by Jonathan Harvey

'Stockhausen: Theory and Music', *Music Review* xxix (1968), 130–41

'Jonathan Harvey writes about his *Persephone Dream*', *The Listener*, lxxix (1973), 58

The Music of Stockhausen, London, 1975

'Composition Teaching at a University', *Composer*, 53–4 (1975), 27–8, 31–2

'Schoenberg, man or woman?', *Music & Letters*, lvi (1975), 371–85

'*Inner Light (3)*', *Musical Times*, cxvii (1976), 125–7

'Brian Ferneyhough', *Musical Times*, cxx (1979), 723–28

'Atonality', *Musical Times*, cxxi (1980), 699–700

'"Mortuos plango, vivos voco": a realization at IRCAM', *Computer Music Journal*, v (1981), 22–4

'Reflection after composition', *Tempo*, 140 (1982), 2–4

'New Directions: a Manifesto', *Soundings*, 11 (1984), 2–13

'Notes on the Realization of Bhakti', *Computer Music Journal*, viii (1984), 74–8

'Electronics in Music: a New Aesthetic?', *Composer*, 85 (1985), 8–15

'Madonna of Winter and Spring', *Musical Times*, cxxvii (1986), 431–3 [1986a]

'The Mirror of Ambiguity', in *The Language of Electro-acoustic Music*, ed. S. Emmerson (London, 1986), 175–90 [1986b]

'IRCAM', in *Pierre Boulez: a Symposium*, ed. W. Glock (London, 1986), 239–46

'An Approach to Church Music', *Musical Times*, cxxxi (1990), 52–5

'Respect for the New', *Musical Times*, cxxxiii (1992), 612

'Sounding out the Inner Self', *Musical Times*, cxxxiii (1992), 613–5

'New Directions: The Conception and Development of a Composition' in *Companion to Contemporary Musical Thought*, ed. J. Paynter et al. (London, 1992), 736–50 [cf. *Soundings* article from 1984, above]

'Foreword', *Brian Ferneyhough: Collected Writings*, ed. J. Boros & R. Toop (Amsterdam, 1995), ix–xii

Music and Inspiration, London, 1999

Writings on Jonathan Harvey

David Brown, 'Jonathan Harvey', *Musical Times*, cix (1968), 808–10

Peter Evans, 'Jonathan Harvey's Recent Works', *Musical Times*, cxvi (1975), 616–9

Paul Griffiths, 'Three Works by Jonathan Harvey', *Contemporary Music Review*, i (1984), 87–109

Paul Griffiths, conversation with Harvey in *New Sounds, New Personalities* (London, 1985), 46–53

Jane Manning, *New Vocal Repertory*, Vol.2 (Oxford, 1998), 284–91 [on *Nachtlied*]

Bayan Northcott, 'Jonathan Harvey', *Music and Musicians*, March 1973, 34–40

John Palmer, 'Structural Strategies and Pitch Gestalt in Harvey's *Bhakti*', *20th Century Music*, v, (1998), 4–24

John Palmer, 'Jonathan Harvey's *Inquest of Love*: The Redemptive Spirit of Art', *20th Century Music*, v, no. 5 (1998), 8–11

John Palmer, 'An Interview with Jonathan Harvey', *20th Century Music*, v, no. 8 (1998), 1–8

John Palmer, 'An Introduction to Jonathan Harvey's *Bhakti*', *20th Century Music*, v, no. 11 (1998), 6–15

Jan Vandenheede, 'Jonathan Harvey's Ritual Melodies', *Interface*, xxi (1992), 149–83

John Winter, 'Jonathan Harvey's Church Music', *Composer*, 84 (1985), 16–21

David Wright, 'Jonathan Harvey at 50', *The Listener*, cv (1989), 44–5